S P O T L I G H T

TULUM

GARY CHANDLER & LIZA PRADO WITH BETH KOHN

Contents

TULUM

TULUM AND SOUTHERN QUINTANA ROO

Tulum has long been favored by travelers who cringe at the splashy resorts and package tourism found in Cancún (and increasingly the Riviera Maya). In that sense, Tulum is a fitting bridge between Quintana Roo's booming northern section and its far-less-traveled south. Tulum has so far managed to avoid the impulse to fill the coast with ever-bigger resorts; prices have

TULUM AND QUINTANA ROO

Highlights

LOOK FOR █ TO FIND RECOMMENDED SIGHTS, ACTIVITIES, DINING, AND LODGING.

█ **Tulum's Southern Beaches:** Mile after mile of powdery white sand, tranquil turquoise water, cozy bungalows peeking out from behind softly bending palm trees: These are the beaches you've been dreaming of and the reason you came to the Caribbean in the first place (page 15).

█ **Cenotes near Tulum:** Sure the ocean reefs are gorgeous, but don't miss a chance to explore these eerie and unforgettable limestone caverns, bristling with stalagmites and stalactites, and filled with the crystalline water of the world's longest underground river system (page 15).

█ **Bahía de la Ascensión:** A huge protected expanse of calm ocean flats and tangled mangrove forests make this a world-class destination for bird-watchers and anglers. Take an all-day tour from Tulum or sit back and stay awhile at a homey lodge or bed-and-breakfast in Punta Allen (page 32).

█ **Banco Chinchorro:** A punishing two-hour boat ride across the open sea is rewarded with spectacular diving on one of the world's largest coral atolls. And now you can stay the night, doubling your diving pleasure (page 48).

█ **Fuerte San Felipe Bacalar:** Housed in a stout star-shaped fort, this small-town museum

has fascinating and innovative displays on piracy and the Caste War. It overlooks beautiful Laguna Bacalar, which the Maya called Lake of Seven Colors (page 54).

certainly gone up, but there are still no mega-developments here, or even power lines for that matter. Its beaches and *cabañas* remain as idyllic as ever.

If Tulum is the anti-Cancún, you might call southern Quintana Roo the non-Cancún. Though fairly close in distance, it's worlds apart by any other measure. Immediately south of Tulum is the massive Sian Ka'an Biosphere Reserve, one of the Yucatán's largest and richest preserves, whose bays, lagoons, mangrove stands, and inland forests support a vast array of plants and animals, from

dolphins to jaguars; there's even a large Maya ruin and several smaller temples. Beyond Sian Ka'an is the "Costa Maya," a fancy term for the sparsely populated stretch of coast reaching down to the Belize border; the largest towns are Mahahual and Xcalak, with numerous small bed-and-breakfasts and seaside hotels in both (and a highly incongruous cruise ship port in Mahahual). Most of the beaches aren't postcard perfect like Tulum's, but the isolation—not to mention the far-less-expensive lodging—are hard to match. Inland and farther south is the multicolored Laguna Bacalar and several

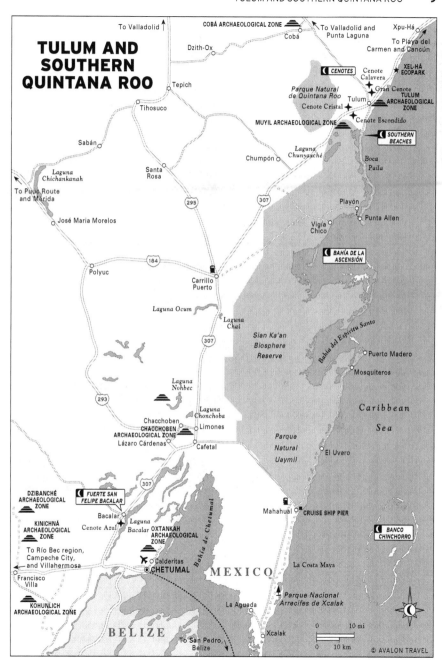

TULUM AND SOUTHERN QUINTANA ROO

To Valladolid

COBÁ ARCHAEOLOGICAL ZONE

Cobá

To Valladolid and
Punta Laguna

Xpu-Há

To Playa del
Carmen and Cancún

Dzith-Ox

CENOTES   Cenote
Calavera

XEL-HÁ
ECOPARK

Tepich

Parque Natural
de Quintana Roo

Gran Cenote

Tulum

TULUM
ARCHAEOLOGICAL
ZONE

Tihosuco

Cenote Cristal

Cenote Escondido

MUYIL ARCHAEOLOGICAL ZONE

SOUTHERN
BEACHES

Sabán

Laguna
Chunyaxché

Boca
Paila

Laguna
Chichankanah

Santa
Rosa

Chumpón

To Puuc Route
and Mérida

295

307

Playón

Punta Allen

José Maria Morelos

Vigía
Chico

184

BAHÍA DE LA
ASCENSIÓN

Polyuc

Carrillo
Puerto

Laguna Ocum

Laguna
Chai

Sian Ka'an
Biosphere
Reserve

Bahía del Espíritu Santo

Puerto Madero

Mosquiteros

293

Laguna
Nohbec

Caribbean

Sea

Chacchoben

CHACCHOBEN
ARCHAEOLOGICAL ZONE

Laguna
Chonchoba

Limones

Lázaro Cárdenas

Cafetal

Parque
Natural
Uaymil

El Uvero

307

DZIBANCHÉ
ARCHAEOLOGICAL
ZONE

FUERTE SAN
FELIPE BACALAR

Mahahual

CRUISE SHIP PIER

KINICHNÁ
ARCHAEOLOGICAL
ZONE

Bacalar

Cenote Azul

Laguna
Bacalar

OXTANKAH
ARCHAEOLOGICAL
ZONE

BANCO
CHINCHORRO

To Río Bec region,
Campeche City,
and Villahermosa

Calderitas

CHETUMAL

La Costa Maya

Francisco
Villa

MEXICO

Bahía de Chetumal

Parque Nacional
Arrecifes de Xcalak

KOHUNLICH
ARCHAEOLOGICAL ZONE

La Agueda

BELIZE

To San Pedro,
Belize

Xcalak

0   10 mi

0   10 km

© AVALON TRAVEL

significant but all-but-forgotten Maya ruins. Chetumal, the state capital, isn't much of a destination itself but has some unexpectedly appealing areas nearby, and is the gateway to Belize.

PLANNING YOUR TIME

Tulum is the first stop, of course, and for many people their main destination. From Tulum you can take day trips or short overnighters to Sian Ka'an reserve and Cobá archaeological site, both fascinating. To venture any farther south you'll probably want a rental car, as bus service grows infrequent. Mahahual and Xcalak are certainly worth savoring; despite their isolation, there's plenty to do in both, including snorkeling, diving, kayaking, fishing, and, of course, just relaxing. Laguna Bacalar is worth a day or possibly two, to take a boat trip on the Caribbean-like water, swim in Cenote Azul, and visit the surprisingly good history museum in town. Chetumal is a logical stopover for those headed west toward the Río Bec region or crossing into Belize, and it has an interesting Maya museum.

Tulum

Tulum is the subject of a thousand postcards, and justly so. It's hard to know if the name is more closely associated with the ancient Maya ruins—perched dramatically on a cliff overlooking the Caribbean—or the idyllic beaches and oceanfront *cabañas* that have long been the jewel of the Riviera Maya. What's certain is that Tulum manages to capture both the ancient mystery and modern allure of Mexico's Riviera Maya.

Tulum has definitely grown and changed, with more changes on the way. The beach used to be a haven for backpackers and bohemians, with simple *cabañas* facing beautiful untouched beaches. The beaches are still beautiful, but the prices have long since gone through the *palapa* roof, catering more to urban escapists and upscale yoga groups. It's still a lovely place to stay, no matter who you are, just not as cheap as it used to be.

One consequence of the spike in prices on the beach is that the inland village of Tulum (aka Tulum Pueblo) has perked up significantly. Long a dumpy roadside town, it now has a growing number of hotels, B&Bs, and recommendable restaurants catering to independent travelers who have been priced out of the beachfront hotels. To be sure, a beachside *cabaña* will always be the most appealing place to stay in Tulum—and there are a handful of bargains still to be had—but staying in town is no longer the huge step down that it once was.

ORIENTATION

The name Tulum is used for three separate areas, which can be confusing. The first is Tulum archaeological zone, the scenic and popular Maya ruins. This is the first part of Tulum you encounter as you drive south from Cancún. A kilometer and a half (1 mile) farther south (and well inland) is the town of Tulum, known as Tulum Pueblo, where you'll find the bus terminal, supermarket, and numerous restaurants, hotels, Internet cafés, and other shops. The third area is Tulum's beachfront hotel zone, or Zona Hotelera. Located due east of Tulum Pueblo, the Zona Hotelera extends for almost 10 kilometers (6 miles) from the Maya ruins to the entrance of the Sian Ka'an Biosphere Reserve, with fantastic beaches and bungalow-style hotels virtually the entire way. There's a walking path, but no road, connecting the Tulum ruins to the upper end of Tulum's Zona Hotelera.

TULUM ARCHAEOLOGICAL ZONE

The Maya ruins of **Tulum** (8am-5pm daily, US$4.75) are one of Mexico's most scenic archaeological sites, built atop a 12-meter

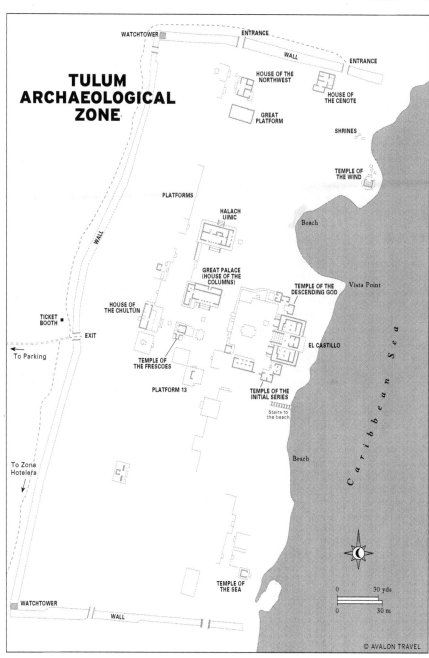

(40-foot) cliff rising abruptly from turquoise Caribbean waters. The structures don't compare in grandeur to those of Cobá, Uxmal, or elsewhere, but are interesting and significant nevertheless.

Tulum is the single most frequently visited Maya ruin in the Yucatán Peninsula, receiving thousands of visitors every day, most on package tours from nearby resorts. (In fact, it's second only to Teotihuacán, near Mexico City, as the country's most-visited archaeological site.) For that reason, the first and most important piece of advice for independent travelers regarding Tulum is to *arrive early.* It used to be that the tour bus madness didn't begin until 11am, but it creeps earlier and earlier every year. Still, if you're there right at 8am, you'll have the ruins mostly to yourself for an hour or so—which is about all you need for this small site—before the hordes descend. Guides can be hired at the entrance for around US$35 for 1-4 people. Bring your swimsuit if you fancy a morning swim: This is the only Maya ruin with a great little beach right inside the archaeological zone.

History

Tulum was part of a series of Maya forts and trading outposts established along the Caribbean coast from the Gulf of Mexico as far south as present-day Honduras. Its original name was Zamá-Xamanzamá or simply Zamá (derived from *zamal,* or dawn) but was later called Tulum, Yucatec Maya for fortification or city wall, in reference to the thick stone barrier that encloses the city's main structures. Measuring 380 by 165 meters (1,250 by 540 feet), it's the largest fortified Maya site on the Quintana Roo coast (though small compared to most inland ruins).

Tulum's enviable patch of seashore was settled as early as 300 BC, but it remained little more than a village for most of its existence, overshadowed by the Maya city of Tankah a few kilometers to the north. Tulum gained prominence between the 12th and 16th centuries (the Late Post-Classic era), when mostly non-Maya immigrants repopulated the Yucatan

Peninsula following the general Maya collapse several centuries prior. Tulum's strategic location and convenient beach landing made it a natural hub for traders, who plied the coast in massive canoes measuring up to 16 meters (52 feet) long, laden with honey, salt, wax, animal skins, vanilla, obsidian, amber, and other products.

It was during this Post-Classic boom period that most of Tulum's main structures were built. Although influenced by Mayapán (the reigning power at the time) and Central Mexican city-states, from which many of Tulum's new residents had emigrated, Tulum's structures mostly exemplify "east coast architecture," defined by austere designs with relatively little ornamentation and a predominantly horizontal orientation (compared to high-reaching pyramids elsewhere). Ironically, construction in these later eras tended to be rather shoddy, thanks in part to improvements in stucco coverings that meant the quality of underlying masonry was not as precise. Today, with the stucco eroded away, Tulum's temples appear more decayed than structures at other sites, even those built hundreds of years prior.

The Spanish got their first view of Tulum, and of mainland indigenous society, on May 7, 1518, when Juan de Grijalva's expedition along the Quintana Roo coast sailed past the then brightly colored fortress. The chaplain of the fleet famously described the city as "a village so large that Seville would not have appeared larger or better." Tulum remained an important city and port until the mid-1500s, when European-borne diseases decimated its population. The once-grand city was effectively abandoned and, for the next three centuries, slowly consumed by coastal vegetation. In 1840, Spanish explorers referred to an ancient walled city known as Tulum, the first recorded use of its current name; two years later the famous American/English team of John Lloyd Stephens and Frederick Catherwood visited Tulum, giving the world its first detailed description and illustrations of the dramatic seaside site. During the Caste

© LIZA PRADO

Archaeologists aren't really sure what purpose these miniature structures (dubbed the "Shrines") at Tulum's Temple of the Wind served.

War, Tulum was occupied by members of the Talking Cross cult, including the followers of a Maya priestess known as the Queen of Tulum.

House of the Cenote

The path from the ticket booth follows Tulum's wall around the northwest corner to two low corbel arch entryways. Using the second entrance (closest to the ocean), you'll first see the Casa del Cenote. The two-room structure, with a third chamber added later, is less impressive than the gaping maw of its namesake cenote. The water is not drinkable, thanks to saltwater intrusion, but that may not have been the case a half millennium ago; it's unlikely Tulum could have grown to its size and prominence without a major water source, not only for its own residents but passing traders as well. Cenotes were also considered apertures to Xibalba, or the underworld, and an elaborate tomb discovered in the floor of the House of the Cenote suggests it may have had a ceremonial function as well.

Temple of the Wind

Following the path, the next major structure is the Temple of the Wind, perched regally atop a rocky outcrop overlooking a picturesque sandy cove. If it looks familiar, that's because it appears on innumerable postcards, magazine photos, and tourist brochures. (The view is even better from a vista point behind El Castillo, and of course from the ocean.) The name derives from the unique circular base upon which the structure is built: In Central Mexican cosmology, the circle is associated with the god of the wind, and its presence here (and at other ruins, like San Gervasio on Isla Cozumel) is evidence of the strong influence that Central Mexican migrants/invaders had on Post-Classic Maya societies.

Temple of the Descending God

One of Tulum's more curious structures is the Temple of the Descending God, named for the upside-down winged figure above its doorway. Exactly who or what the figure represents is disputed among archaeologists—theories include Venus, the setting sun, the god of rain, even the god of bees (as honey was one of the coastal Maya's most widely traded products). Whatever the answer, it was clearly a deeply revered (or feared) deity, as the same image appears on several of Tulum's buildings, including the upper temple of Tulum's main pyramid. The Temple of the Descending God also is notable for its cartoonish off-kilter position, most likely the result of poor construction.

El Castillo

Tulum's largest and most imposing structure is The Castle, a 12-meter-high (40-foot) pyramid constructed on a rocky bluff of roughly the same height. Like many Maya structures, El Castillo was built in multiple phases. The first iteration was a low broad platform, still visible today, topped by a long palace fronted by a phalanx of stout columns. The second phase consisted of simply filling in the center portion of the original palace to create a base for a new and loftier temple on top. In the process, the builders created a vaulted passageway and inner chamber, in which a series of intriguing frescoes were housed; unfortunately, you're not allowed to climb onto the platform to see them. The upper temple (also off-limits) displays Central Mexican influence, including snakelike columns similar to those found at Chichén Itzá and grimacing Toltec masks on the corners. Above the center door is an image of the Descending God. Archaeologists believe a stone block at the top of the stairs may have been used for sacrifices.

Temple of the Frescoes

Though quite small, the Temple of the Frescoes is considered one of Tulum's most archaeologically significant structures. The name owes to the fading but remarkably detailed paintings on the structure's inner walls. In shades of blue, gray, and black, they depict various deities, including Chaac (the god of rain) and Ixchel (the goddess of the moon and fertility), and a profusion of symbolic imagery, including corn and flowers. On the temple's two facades are carved figures with elaborate headdresses and yet another image of the Descending God. The large grim-faced masks on the temple's corners are believed to represent Izamná, the Maya creator god.

Halach Uinic and the Great Palace

In front of El Castillo are the remains of two palatial structures: the House of the Halach Uinic and the Great Palace (also known as the House of the Columns). Halach Uinic is a Yucatec Maya term for king or ruler, and this structure seems to have been an elaborate shrine dedicated to Tulum's enigmatic Descending God. The building is severely deteriorated, but what remains suggests its facade was highly ornamented, perhaps even painted blue and red. Next door is the Great Palace, which likely served as residential quarters for Tulum's royal court.

Practicalities

Tulum's massive parking lot and strip-mall-like visitors complex ought to clue you in to the number of tourists that pass through here every day. (Did we mention to get here early?) You'll find a small museum and bookshop amid innumerable souvenir shops and fast-food restaurants. (If this is your first visit to a Maya ruin, don't be turned off by all the hubbub. Tulum is unique for its excessive and obnoxious commercialization; most sites have just a ticket booth and restrooms.)

The actual entrance and ticket booth are about one kilometer (0.6 mile) from the visitors center; it's a flat mild walk, but there are also **trolleys** that ferry guests back and forth for US$2.25 per person round-trip (kids under 10 ride free).

Getting There

The Tulum archaeological zone is a kilometer (0.6 mile) north of Tulum Pueblo on Highway 307. There are two entrances; the one farther south is newer and better, leading directly to the main parking lot (parking US$4). Arriving by bus or *combi,* be sure to ask the driver to let you off at *las ruínas* (the ruins) as opposed to the town. To return, flag down a bus or *combi* on the highway.

BEACHES AND CENOTES
Northern Beaches
The road from Tulum Pueblo hits the coast near the upper end of the Zona Hotelera, which stretches from the archaeological zone down to the entrance of Sian Ka'an reserve, almost exactly 10 kilometers (6 miles). The area north of the Tulum/Zona Hotelera junction has two easy-to-reach beach areas that are ideal for people staying in town.

Playa El Paraíso (Carr. Tulum-Punta Allen, 2 kilometers/1.2 miles north of junction, cell. tel. 984/113-7089, www.elparaisotulum.com, 8am-6pm daily, beach bar 8pm-midnight Thurs.-Sat.) is a popular beach club on a scenic beach of the same name. Once little more than a bar and some hammocks, the beach club has grown popular with tour groups and has morphed into a bustling expanse of lounge chairs, beach beds, and umbrellas (US$2-20/day), with waiters weaving between them. There's a full restaurant and beach bar, and the nearby water sports center offers snorkeling, diving, kiteboarding, and more. It's busy but still scenic and relaxing.

Directly north of Playa El Paraíso is **Playa Mar Caribe,** named after the rustic bungalows that have long fronted this portion of beach. Broad and unspoiled, this is a great place to come to lay out your towel on the soft white sand, which you share with a picturesque array of moored fishing boats. There are no services here, so be sure to bring snacks and plenty of water. (In a pinch, there's a restaurant at the neighboring beach club.)

(Southern Beaches
Tulum's very best beaches—thick white sand, turquoise-blue water, gently bending palm trees—are toward the southern end of the Zona Hotelera. Not surprisingly, Tulum's finest hotels are in the same area, and there are no official public access points. That said, hotels rarely raise an eyebrow at the occasional nonguest cutting through to reach the beach. You can also grab breakfast or lunch at one of the hotel restaurants and cut down to the beach afterward; in some cases, you can even use the lounge chairs.

Aimed at a mellow upscale crowd, **Ana y José Beach Club** (Carr. Tulum-Punta Allen, 2.4 kilometers/1.5 miles south of junction, no phone, www.anayjosebeachclub.com, 10am-6pm daily, free) is located about a kilometer north of the resort of the same name and is open to guests and nonguests alike. An airy sand-floored dining area serves mostly seafood, including ceviche, shrimp cocktail, and grilled fish, at decent prices and has a full bar. Chaise lounges and four-poster beach beds (US$5-15/day) are arranged a bit too close together, but they are comfy and relaxing nonetheless. Monday and Tuesday are the least crowded.

(Cenotes
Once a modest roadside operation, **Hidden Worlds** (Hwy. 307 Km. 115, toll-free Mex. tel. 800/681-6755, toll-free U.S. tel. 888/339-8001, www.hiddenworlds.com, 9am-sunset daily, last tour leaves at 2pm) is now a full-blown package tourist attraction, and part of the international Rainforest Adventures company. It remains a great introduction to underground snorkeling or diving, with a gorgeous on-site cenote system, frequent departures, and a staff that's accustomed to first-timers. A basic snorkeling tour (1 cenote, 1.5 hours) runs US$35, while one-tank dives are US$135; both including gear. The ever-growing list of nondiving attractions, including ziplines and rappelling, plus combo tours like "Ultimate Adventure + CoCoBongo," make this a fun destination for the whole family but detract somewhat from the underwater options.

Dos Ojos (Hwy. 307 Km. 117, tel. 984/877-8535, www.cenotedosojos.com, 8am-5pm daily) is located just north of Hidden Worlds but is far less commercialized. Dos Ojos, or Two Eyes, is a reference to twin caverns that are the largest openings—but far from the

one of Tulum's utterly perfect southern beaches

© LIZA PRADO

only ones—into the labyrinthine river system that runs beneath the ground here. You can snorkel on your own (US$10), but you'll see a lot more on a guided snorkeling tour (US$40 pp, no reservations required); be sure to ask to visit the Bat Cave. After the tour, you're free to keep snorkeling on your own; in fact, there are hammocks and benches, so you can bring food and drinks and make a day of it. Diving trips (US$130 for 2 tanks, maximum 4 divers per guide) should be arranged in advance. It's two kilometers (1.2 miles) from the entrance to the cenotes, so a rental car is handy. Discounts are available if you have your own gear.

Other favorite cenotes include **Zazil Ha, Car Wash/Aktun Ha, Gran Cenote,** and **Calavera Cenote** (all west of Tulum on the road to Cobá); **Cristal** and **Escondido** (Hwy. 307 just south of Tulum); **Casa Cenote** (at Tankah Tres); **Cenote Azul** and **Cristalina** (Hwy. 307 across from Xpu-Há); and **Chac Mol** (Hwy. 307, 2 kilometers/1.2 miles north of Xpu-Há). All can be visited on a tour or by

yourself, and most have snorkel gear for rent (US$6-8). Most are on private or *ejido* (collective) land and charge admission fees, usually US$3.50-6 for snorkelers and US$8.50 for divers. If you take a tour, ask if admission fees are included in the rate. Most cenotes are open 8am-5pm daily.

TOURS OF SIAN KA'AN BIOSPHERE RESERVE

CESiaK (Hwy. 307 just south of the Tulum ruins turnoff, tel. 984/871-2499, www.cesiak. org, 8am-2pm and 4pm-8pm daily) is a long-standing nonprofit group offering excellent tours of the Sian Ka'an Biosphere, a 1.3-million-acre reserve of coastal and mangrove forests and wetlands, with pristine coral reefs and a huge variety of flora and fauna. The most popular is the "Canal Tour," a six-hour excursion (US$78 pp) that includes taking a motorboat tour of the several lagoons, including stops to see a small Maya ruin and float down a mangrove canal. The late afternoon "Canal & Birdwatching" tour (US$78 pp)

© LIZA PRADO

Despite being deep underground, most of the Riviera Maya's popular cenotes are quite accessible, with stairways and interior lighting.

includes a boat tour of three bird-rich lagoons and a stop at the aptly named San Miguel Bird Island, or you can go by kayak (US$50, 3 hours). Most tours include hotel pickup, lunch or dinner, and a bilingual guide.

Community Tours Sian Ka'an (Calle Osiris Sur near Calle Sol Ote, tel. 984/871-2202 or cell. tel. 984/114-0750, www.siankaantours. org, 7am-9pm daily) is an excellent community-run agency offering a variety of Sian Ka'an tours, such as the Muyil route (US$99 pp, 7 hours), which begins with a visit to Muyil archaeological zone, then a boat tour of Muyil and Chunyaxche lagoons, including a chance to jump in and float down a long mangrove-edged canal; "Mayaking" in Sian Ka'an (US$45pp, 3 hours), a bird- and animal-spotting tour by kayak through the lagoons and mangroves; and a "Chicle" tour (US$99, 6 hours), where you learn about the practice of tapping *chicle* (gum) trees, from Maya times to today, followed by a swim in the lagoon.

ENTERTAINMENT AND SHOPPING
Entertainment

In the Zona Hotelera, the lounge bar at **La Zebra** (Carr. Tulum-Punta Allen, 4.8 kilometers/3 miles south of junction, cell. tel. 984/115-4726, www.lazebratulum.com) serves up shots and mixed drinks, including its signature Zebra margarita, made with pineapple and ginger and served on the rocks. On Sunday, it hosts a salsa party from 8pm to midnight, with a free dance class at 6pm. Dinner reservations are recommended if you want to feast on pulled-pork tacos between sets.

Papaya Playa Project (Carr. Tulum-Punta Allen, 1.5 kilometers/1 mile south of junction, cell. tel. 984/116-3774, www.papayaplayaproject) has a regular lineup of live musical acts, plus full-moon parties, bongo drum sessions, and an overall counterculture vibe. Saturdays are the main night, but look for schedules online or around town for upcoming events. Papaya Playa is actually a rustic-chic resort, hence all the *cabañas,* but is better known (and better liked, really) as a place to party. Most shows begin around 10pm; cover is US$5-10.

The upscale boutique resort **Mezzanine** (Carr. Tulum-Punta Allen, 1.3 kilometers/0.8 mile north of junction, cell. tel. 984/113-1596, www.mezzaninetulum.com) is known as the go-to bar on Friday nights, with cool cocktails and a hip vibe.

In Tulum Pueblo, **El Curandero** (Av. Tulum at Calle Beta, no phone, www.curanderotulum. com, 7pm-3am Mon.-Tues. and Thurs.-Sat.) is one of several local bars cut from the same cloth: small, mood lit, with great music and a relaxed vibe. Hookahs have become a popular feature in bars in the Riviera Maya, including Tulum. El Curandero has live music weekdays (except Wednesday), electronica on Saturday, and movies on Thursday.

Waye'Rest-Bar (Av. Tulum btwn Calles Beta and Osiris) and **Pepero** (Av. Tulum btwn Calles Jupiter and Acuario) are alternatives.

Shopping

Mixik Artesanía (Av. Tulum btwn Calles Alfa and Jupiter, tel. 984/871-2136, 9am-9pm Mon.-Sat.) has a large selection of quality folk art, from green copper suns to carved wooden angels and masks. Cool T-shirts, jewelry, cards, and more also are sold. There's a sister shop of the same name in the Zona Hotelera.

Casa Hernández (Av. Tulum at Calle Centauro, no phone, 9am-5pm daily except Thurs.) specializes in handcrafted pottery and ceramics, mostly from Puebla. Items range from mugs and picture frames to finely painted plates and dinner sets.

SPORTS AND RECREATION
Scuba Diving

The reef here is superb, but Tulum's diving claim to fame is the huge and easily accessible network of freshwater cenotes, caverns, and caves, offering truly one-of-a-kind dive environments. Divers with open-water certification can dive in cenotes (little or no overhead) and caverns (no more than 30 feet deep or 130 feet from an air pocket) without additional training. Full-cave diving requires advanced certification, which is also available at many of Tulum's shops. If you haven't dived in a while, definitely warm up with some open-water dives before doing a cenote or cavern trip. Buoyancy control is especially important in such environments because of the roof above and the sediment below, and is complicated by the fact that it's freshwater instead of saltwater, and entails gear you may not be accustomed to, namely thick wetsuits and a flashlight.

Prices for cenotes and caverns are fairly uniform from shop to shop: around US$75-110 for one tank or US$95-130 for two. Be sure to ask whether gear and admission to the cenotes are included. Shops also offer multidive packages, cave and cavern certification courses, and hotel packages if you'll be staying awhile. As always, choose a shop and guide you feel comfortable with, not necessarily the least-expensive one.

If you plan on doing as much cave and cavern diving as possible, **Xibalba Dive Center & Hotel** (Calle Andrómeda btwn Calles Libra and Geminis, tel. 984/871-2953, www.xibalbahotel.com, 9am-7pm daily) not only has an excellent record for safety and professionalism, but now has an on-site hotel with comfortable rooms, a small swimming pool, and space to dry, store, and repair gear. Good lodging and diving packages are available. Xibalba also fills its own tanks, and offers free Nitrox to experienced clients. The shop's name, aptly enough, comes from the Yucatec Maya word for the underworld.

Koox Dive Center (Av. Tulum btwn Calles Beta and Osiris, cell. tel. 984/118-7031, www. kooxdiving.com, 9am-sunset daily) shares a shop with a popular kiteboarding outfit, and is another reliable option for diving and snorkeling, on the reef and in cenotes.

Mot Mot Diving (Av. Tulum at Calle Beta, cell. tel. 984/151-4718, www.motmotdiving. com, 9am-9pm daily) is recommended by several hotel owners.

Cenote Dive Center (Calle Centauro at Calle Andrómeda, tel. 984/876-3285, www. cenotedive.com, 8am-4pm Sun.-Fri.) offers a large variety of tours and courses, in Tulum and beyond.

In the Zona Hotelera, **Mexi-Divers** (Carr. Tulum-Punta Allen Km. 5, tel. 984/807-8805, www.mexidivers.com, 8:30am-5pm daily) is located opposite Zamas Hotel in the Punta Piedra area and has regularly scheduled snorkeling and diving trips, in the ocean and nearby cenotes, at somewhat lower prices.

Dos Ojos (tel. 984/877-8535, www.cenotedosojos.com, 8am-5pm daily) and **Hidden Worlds** (toll-free Mex. tel. 800/681-6755, toll-free U.S. tel. 888/339-8001, www.hiddenworlds.com, 9am-sunset daily, last tour leaves at 2pm) are located north of town and also offer excellent diving tours.

Snorkeling

Like divers, snorkelers have an embarrassment of riches in Tulum, with great reef snorkeling and easy access to the eerie beauty of the area's many cenotes. **Dive shops in Tulum** offer snorkel trips of both sorts; prices vary considerably so be sure to ask which and how many reefs or cenotes you'll visit, for how long, and what's included (gear, entrance fees, transport, snacks, etc.). Reef trips cost US$25-40 visiting 1-3 different spots, while cenote trips run US$45-70; snorkel gear can also be rented. North of Tulum, **Hidden Worlds** (toll-free Mex. tel. 800/681-6755, toll-free U.S. tel. 888/339-8001, www.hiddenworlds.com, 9am-sunset daily, last tour leaves at 2pm) and **Dos Ojos** (tel. 984/877-8535, www.cenotedosojos.com, 8am-5pm daily) both offer excellent cenote snorkeling tours for US$35-40; Hidden Worlds has a lot of extras, like rappelling and ziplines, while Dos Ojos allows you to snorkel on your own—all day if you like—after the tour is over.

Kiteboarding

Extreme Control (Av. Tulum btwn Calles Beta and Osiris, tel. 984/745-4555, www.extremecontrol.net, 9am-sunset daily) is Tulum's longest-operating kiteboarding outfit, offering courses and rentals for all experience levels and in various languages. Most classes are held at

Playa El Paraíso Beach Club, north of the junction, where it also has an info kiosk. Private classes are US$72 per hour, or US$216-432 for three- to six-hour introductory packages, including equipment; group classes are somewhat less.

Morph Kiteboarding (cell. tel. 984/114-9524, www.morphkiteboarding.com) offers classes by IKO-certified instructors to all levels of kiteboarders. Rates are for private classes, though group lessons can be arranged as well: US$225, US$395, and US$420 for three-, five-, and six-hour courses, respectively. Rates include hotel pickup and transportation to the nearest kiting beach.

Ocean Pro Kite (Akiin Beach Club, Carr. Tulum-Punta Allen Km. 9.5, cell. tel. 984/119-0328, www.oceanprokite.com) is another option.

Stand-Up Paddling

Stand-up paddling, or "SUPing," has exploded in popularity, a challenging but relatively easy sport to master, and especially well-suited to the calm clear waters found in much of the Riviera Maya. You can see a surprising amount of sealife doing SUP instead of kayaking, thanks simply to the improved vantage point.

Ocean Pro Kite (Akiin Beach Club, Carr. Tulum-Punta Allen Km. 9.5, tel. 984/876-3263 or cell. tel. 984/119-0328, www.oceanprokite.com) offers SUP lessons for all levels, starting with safety and theory on the beach, graduating to kneeling paddling, then standing and catching waves. Private classes are US$60 per hour or US$120 half day, while groups of two or three start at US$40 per person per hour. Gear, guide, transport, and refreshments are all included.

Extreme Control (Av. Tulum btwn Calles Beta and Osiris, tel. 984/745-4555, www.extremecontrol.net, 9am-sunset daily) also offers SUPing lessons (US$70 private, US$50 pp 2 pax, US$35 pp 3+ pax; 2 hours) plus tours, rentals, and transport to and from Tulum, Akumal, and Tankah. Its office in town is convenient for information and booking.

Ecoparks

Built around a huge natural inlet, **Xel-Há** (Hwy. 307, 9 kilometers/5.6 miles north of Tulum, cell. tel. 984/105-6981, www.xel-ha. com, 8:30am-6pm daily, US$79 adult all-inclusive, US$119 adult with round-trip transportation, child under 12 half off, child under 5 free) is all about being in and around the water. Activities include snorkeling, snuba, tubing, and interactive programs with dolphins, manatees, and stingrays. Although it doesn't compare to snorkeling on the reef, there's a fair number of fish darting about, and it makes for a fun, easy intro for children and beginners. Check the website for online deals and combo packages with sister resorts Xcaret and Xplor.

Bicycling

In Tulum town, **Iguana Bike Shop** (Av. Satélite near Calle Andrómeda, tel. 984/871-2357 or cell. tel. 984/119-0836, www.iguanabike. com, 9am-7pm Mon.-Sat.) offers mountain bike tours to snorkeling sites at various cenotes

© GARY CHANDLER

Tulum is known for its whimsy and artfulness, including murals like this one.

and beaches, as well as turtle nesting grounds on Xcacel beach. Prices vary depending on the tour; they typically last four hours and are limited to six cyclists.

Spas

Overlooking the beach at Copal hotel, **Maya Spa Wellness Center** (Carr. Tulum-Punta Allen Km. 5, toll-free Mex. tel. 800/681-9537, www.maya-spa.com, 8am-8pm daily) offers a variety of massages, facials, and body wraps in a gorgeous setting. Massages run US$100 to US$150 (60-80 minutes), while other treatments average US$60 (1 hour).

Located at the Ana y José hotel, **Om... Spa** (Carr. Tulum-Punta Allen Km. 7, tel. 984/871-2477, ext. 202, www.anayjose.com, 9am-5pm daily) is a full-service spa set in a chic beachfront setting. Choose from a menu of massages (US$80-100) and body treatments (US$60-100).

Yoga

Surrounded by lush vegetation, **Yoga Shala Tulum** (Carr. Tulum-Punta Allen Km. 4.4, cell. tel. 984/137-3016, www.yogashalatulum.com, 7am-6pm Mon.-Sat., 4:30pm-6pm Sun.) offers a wide range of yoga instruction in its gorgeous open-air studio. Classes cost US$15 each or US$50 per week for unlimited classes. There also is an affordable hotel on-site. Look for it on the inland side of the Zona Hotelera road.

Maya Spa Wellness Center (Carr. Tulum-Punta Allen Km. 5, toll-free Mex. tel. 800/681-9537, www.maya-spa.com, 8am-8pm daily) also offers yoga sessions.

ACCOMMODATIONS

Chances are you've come to Tulum to stay in one of the famous beachside bungalow-type hotels. There are many to choose from, each slightly different but most sharing a laid-back atmosphere and terrific beaches. However, some travelers are surprised by just how rustic some accommodations are, even those charging hundreds of dollars per night. The root of the matter is that there are no power lines or freshwater wells serving the beach. Virtually all accommodations have salty water in the showers and sinks. Most have fans, but not all, and electricity may be limited to nighttime hours only. Air-conditioning is available in only a handful of places. At the same time, some hotels use generators to power their restaurants and reception, so it's worth asking for a room away from the generator; nothing is a bigger killjoy than a diesel motor pounding outside your window when the point of coming here was to enjoy the peace and quiet.

If staying on the beach is out of your budget (join the club!), staying in town is a perfectly good alternative. The options have improved significantly, with a crop of new bed-and-breakfasts and boutique hotels to go along with longtime hostels and budget digs. The beach is just a short drive or bike ride away, and prices for food, Internet, and laundry are much lower.

Zona Hotelera
UNDER US$100
A private home turned yoga hotel, **Yoga Shala Tulum** (Carr. Tulum-Punta Allen Km. 4.4, cell. tel. 984/137-3016, www.yogashalatulum.com, US$49/69 s/d with shared bath, US$79/89 s/d) offers simple but comfortable rooms on a jungly plot on the inland side of the Zona Hotelera. Rooms have whitewashed walls, polished cement floors, and good beds and linens, with a bit of boho flair, too. Outside is an impressive open-air yoga studio with a high *palapa* roof and gorgeous wood floors.

Ahau Tulum (Carr. Tulum-Punta Allen Km. 4.4, cell. tel. 984/167-1154 or 984/144-3348, www.ahautulum.com, US$29-99 s/d) is not exclusively a budget place—it's got rooms that go for over US$400—but its guesthouse units (with shared bathrooms) and stick-built "Bali Huts" are among the cheapest digs on the beach. Gaps in the walls and bathrooms that never get truly clean are the price you pay to be on the sand for this cheap—a bargain for boho beachhounds.

US$100-200
Although sharing a bathroom for $100 doesn't seem quite right, **Coco Tulum** (Carr.

Tulum-Punta Allen Km. 7, cell. tel. 984/157-4830, www.cocotulum.com, US$79-98 s/d with shared bath, US$125-195 s/d) does the basics with style. Tidy *palapa*-roofed bungalows have cement floors, comfy beds, hanging bookshelfs, fans, and sleek black exteriors. The shared bathrooms are actually quite nice, with modern basin sinks, rainshower heads, hot water, and thrice-daily cleaning. And if sharing a bathroom really is beyond the pale, they've got a tower with three deluxe rooms, each with private bathroom, fan, and stellar views. Wind- and solar-powered electricity is available 24 hours.

Accommodations at the lovely and well-liked **Cabañas La Luna** (Carr. Tulum-Punta Allen Km. 6.5, U.S. tel. 818/631-9824, Mex. cell. tel. 984/146-7737 [urgent matters only], www.cabanaslaluna.com, US$160-300 s/d, US$550 two- and four-bedroom villas) range from cozy beachfront bungalows to spacious split-level villas, but share essential details like comfortable mattresses, high ceilings, fans and 24-hour electricity, and bright artful decor. The beach is stunning, of course, and the property is big enough for a sense of isolation, yet within walking distance of shops and restaurants in Punta Piedra. Service is excellent.

Tita Tulum (Carr. Tulum-Punta Allen Km. 8, tel. 984/877-8513, www.titatulum.com, US$160-190 s/d) has a lovely beachfront and low-key atmosphere—a great option for families and travelers who prefer modest comforts and a lower rate (especially off-season) over boutique eco-chic embellishments. Ten guest rooms form a semicircle around a sandy palm-fringed lot; they're a bit worn around the edges but have polished cement floors, clean bathrooms, and indoor and outdoor sitting areas, plus fans, Wi-Fi, and 24-hour electricity. Tita is a charming and attentive proprietor, and prepares authentic Mexican dishes in the hotel's small restaurant.

Posada Lamar (Carr. Tulum-Punta Allen Km. 6, cell. tel. 984/106-3682, www.posadalamar.com, US$125-195 s/d) has eight comfortable and artful bungalows, with salvaged-wood detailing and rich colors and fabrics. There

TULUM TOWN AND ZONA HOTELERA

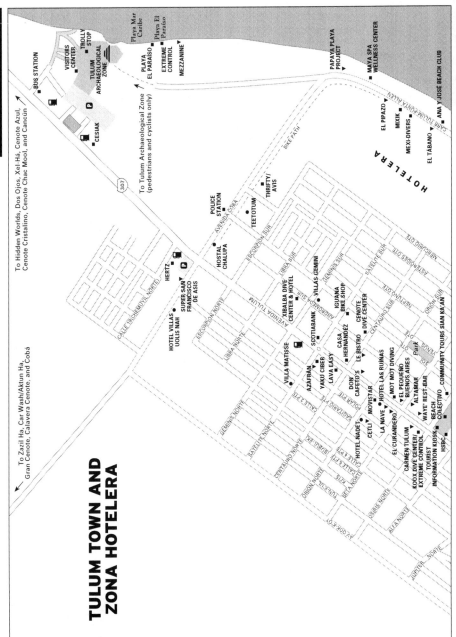

To Zazil Ha, Car Wash/Aktun Ha, Gran Cenote, Calavera Cenote, and Cobá

To Hidden Worlds, Dos Ojos, Xel-Há, Cenote Azul, Cenote Cristalino, Cenote Chac Mool, and Cancún

307

BUS STATION

VISITORS CENTER

TROLLY STOP

TULUM ARCHAEOLOGICAL ZONE

CESIAK

Playa Mar Caribe

Playa El Paraíso

PLAYA EL PARAÍSO

EXTREME CONTROL

MEZZANINE

PAPAYA PLAYA PROJECT

MAYA SPA WELLNESS CENTER

EL PIPAZO

MIXIK

MEXI-DIVERS

EL TABANO

ANA Y JOSÉ BEACH CLUB

CALLE TULUM-PUNTA ALLEN

HOTELERA

MERCURIO OTE

To Tulum Archaeological Zone (pedestrians and cyclists only)

BIKE PATH

POLICE STATION

AVENIDA COBÁ

TEETOTUM

THRIFTY/ AVIS

HOSTAL CHALUPA

HERTZ

SUPER SAN FRANCISCO DE ASIS

HOTEL VILLAS UOLIS NAH

CALLE 19/CHEMUYIL NORTE

ESCORPIÓN NORTE

LIBRA NORTE

ESCORPIÓN SUR

LIBRA SUR

AVENIDA TULUM

ANDRÓMEDA SUR

GÉMINIS SUR

SATÉLITE SUR

CENTAURO SUR

NEPTUNO OTE

ORIÓN OTE

ASTERIDES OTE

XIBALBA DIVE CENTER & HOTEL

VILLAS GÉMINI

IGUANA BIKE SHOP

CENOTE DIVE CENTER

SCOTIABANK

CASA HERNÁNDEZ

LE BISTRO

VILLA MATISSE

AZAFRÁN

YAKU CIBER

LAVA EASY

DON CAFETO'S

Park

MOT MOT DIVING

EL PEQUEÑO BUENOS AIRES

ALTAMAR

WAVE REST-BAR

BEACH COLECTIVO

COMMUNITY TOURS SIAN KA'AN

POLAR BITE

SAGITARIO PTE

CALLE 2 PTE

GÉMINIS NORTE

SATÉLITE NORTE

CENTAURO NORTE

CENTAURO PTE

TUNKUL NORTE

BELA NORTE

KUS

CALLE 6 PTE

CALLE 4 PTE

ORIÓN NORTE

OSIRIS NORTE

ALFA NORTE

JUPITER NORTE

AV CORE K GT

CETLI

LA NAVE

HOTEL LAS RUINAS

EL CURANDERO

CARMEN TULUM

KOOX DIVE CENTER/ EXTREME CONTROL

TOURIST INFORMATION KIOSK

HSBC

HOTEL NADET

MOVISTAR

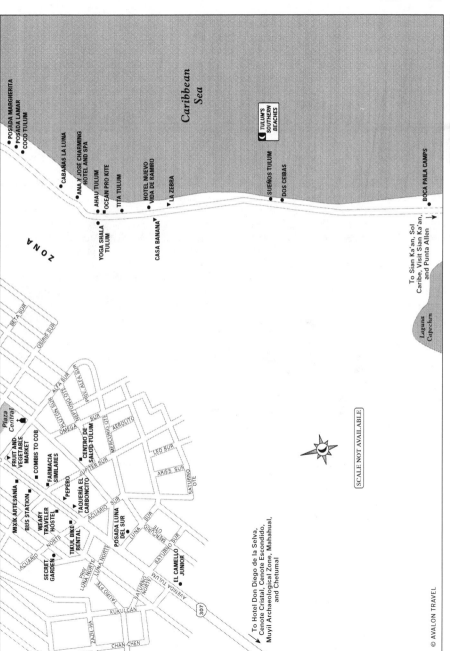

Caribbean Sea

ZONA

TULUM'S SOUTHERN BEACHES

POSADA MARGHERITA
POSADA LAMAR
COCO TULUM
CABAÑAS LA LUNA
ANA Y JOSÉ CHARMING HOTEL AND SPA
AHAU TULUM
OCEAN PRO KITE
YOGA SHALA TULUM
TITA TULUM
HOTEL NUEVO VIDA DE RAMIRO
CASA BANANA
LA ZEBRA
SUEÑOS TULUM
DOS CEIBAS
BOCA PAILA CAMPS

To Sian Ka'an, Sol Caribe, Visit Sian Ka'an, and Punta Allen

Laguna Cabechen

Plaza Central
FRUIT AND VEGETABLE MARKET
COMBIS TO COB
CENTRO DE SALUD TULUM
FARMACIA SIMILARES
PEPERO
MIXIK ARTESANIA
BUS STATION
WEARY TRAVELER HOSTEL
TAQUERIA EL CARBONCITO
TIKUL BIKE RENTAL
POSADA LUNA DEL SUR
SECRET GARDEN
EL CAMELLO JUNIOR

BETA SUR
OSIRIS SUR
PRIV. ALFA SUR
ORUITOS SUR
OMEGA
NEPTUNO OTE
NEPTUNO OTE
PRIV. ALFA SUR
MERCURIO OTE
MERCURIO AEROLITO
JUPITER SUR
LEO SUR
ARIES SUR
SATURNO OTE
ACUARIO SUR
SATURNO SUR
LUNA SUR
ORION SUR
MERCURIO SUR
LUNA
SATURNO SUR
ACUARIO
LUNA NORTE
NORTE
PRIV. LUNA NORTE
TAURO PTE.
PRIV. LUNA NORTE
SATURNO NORTE
AVENIDA TULUM
KUKULCAN
ZAZIL HA
CHAN-CHEN

307

To Hotel Don Diego de la Selva, Cenote Cristal, Cenote Escondido, Muyil Archaeological Zone, Mahahual, and Chetumal

SCALE NOT AVAILABLE

© AVALON TRAVEL

are no fans or air-conditioning, and electricity (solar powered) is available only at night; fortunately the sea breezes keep the units cool (and the bugs at bay) most nights. The bungalows are a bit too close together, diminishing privacy, especially since you often need the windows and doors open, but the beach here is clean and beautiful, with plenty of chairs, beds, and *palapas*. Continental breakfast is included, served every morning on your private terrace.

Dos Ceibas (Carr. Tulum-Punta Allen Km. 10, tel. 984/877-6024, www.dosceibas.com, US$80-170 s/d) has eight comfortable, if a bit garish, bungalows on a beautiful stretch of beach. Bungalows range from a top-floor honeymoon unit to a "bargain" bungalow with a detached bathroom (and near enough the road to hear passing cars). Most have polished cement floors, brightly painted walls, and firm beds with mosquito nets hanging from the *palapa* roof; all but the two breezy oceanfront rooms and budget rear unit have ceiling fans (electricity available at night only).

OVER US$200
Nestled in a wonderfully jungly plot, **(Hotel Nueva Vida de Ramiro** (Carr. Tulum-Punta Allen Km. 8.5, tel. 984/877-8512, www.tulumnv.com, US$105-345 s/d) has a large number (and variety) of accommodations, from spacious suites with pillow-top mattresses and gorgeous ocean views to simple thatch-roof bungalows, including some with kitchenette, and even an adults-only area. (The oldest rooms can be dark, however, and aren't a great value, despite being cheaper.) There's 24-hour clean power, but no air-conditioning, just fans and sea breezes. The beach here is glorious, and the hotel's restaurant, Casa Banana, is located across the street and well-recommended for tasty, affordable meals.

Artful, spirit-minded decor is nothing new in Tulum, but **(Sueños Tulum** (Carr. Tulum-Punta Allen Km. 8.5, tel. 984/876-2152 or cell. tel. 984/115-4338, www.suenostulum.com, US$220-285 s/d) takes the theme further than most. Each of the hotel's 12 suites is decorated according to an essential force—Earth, Rain,

Moon, etc.—and there's Maya imagery inside and out. All have ceiling fans, most rooms have ocean views, and two are reserved for families. A small clean pool is an added bonus, even with beaches as gorgeous as these. Located at the far southern end of the hotel zone, Sueños is quiet and isolated, even by Tulum's standards.

Beachy and hip, **Posada Margherita** (Carr. Tulum-Punta Allen Km. 4.5, tel. 984/801-8493, www.posadamargherita.com, US$208 s/d) has just eight rooms, all boasting stone-inlaid showers, private patio or terrace, and intriguing art from around the world. The beach here is lovely, and the hotel has a restaurant and lounge area just steps from the sand. Posada Margherita runs on solar energy, which means 24 hours of silent electricity. And the restaurant here is not to be missed; it's pricey but one of the best in Tulum.

Ana y José Charming Hotel and Spa (Carr. Tulum-Punta Allen Km. 7, tel. 998/889-6022 reservations or 984/871-2476 reception, www.anayjose.com, US$390-620 s/d) was one of the first resorts in Tulum to offer air-conditioning, a swimming pool, and hotel-style rooms. Though sacrilege to some—and now they're adding TVs!—Ana y José has long been a favorite of those who love Tulum's beaches and isolation, but not so much the beach bungalow, mosquito-net, eco-chic thing. Rooms vary from comfortable doubles, to romantic ocean-view suites, to large family apartments, most with niceties like marble floors, basin sinks, and flower petals on the bed. The inflated prices are for air-conditioning. The beach and spa are lovely, of course, and Ana y José is popular for weddings.

In Town
UNDER US$50
A stylish hostel with a laid-back vibe, **(Hostal Chalupa** (Av. Cobá near Av. Tulum, cell. tel. 984/871-2116, www.chalupatulum.com.mx, US$17 s dorm with a/c, US$21 d dorm with a/c, US$42/50 d/q with a/c) offers air-conditioned dorms with en suite bathrooms and good mattresses; private rooms are similar in look and comfort and sleep up to four. There's

an inviting pool on the ground floor and a large rooftop solarium; movies are shown most nights at 8pm. The community kitchen is vegetarian-only. It's located just outside town, on the road toward the beach; bikes are available for rent (US$4.25/day).

Villa Matisse (Av. Satélite at Calle Sagitario, tel. 984/871-2636, shuvinito@yahoo.com, US$50 s/d) has six simple, comfortable rooms, a pleasant garden and reading area (with book exchange), and a community kitchen. The rooms are spotless, and the grounds and common areas are equally well maintained; the multilingual owner sets out coffee and small snacks in the morning and often supplies rooms with fresh flowers. There's no air-conditioning, but rooms have fans and good cross ventilation. Use of the hotel's bikes is included in the rate.

Hotel Las Ruínas (Av. Tulum btwn Calles Orion and Beta, cell. tel. 984/125-5506, US$50 s/d) won't win any awards for marketing (The Ruins Hotel?) but it does just fine as a budget option for non-hostellers. Rooms are plain and a bit dark, but reasonably clean and comfortable, with air-conditioning and TVs. No Wi-Fi, but there's an Internet café at the corner. The hotel is run by a friendly family who live on-site.

US$50-100

Tucked into a quiet residential street, **C Secret Garden** (Calle Sagitario near Calle Acuario, tel. 984/804-3697, www.secretgardentulum.com, US$50-60 s/d with a/c, US$70 s/d with a/c and kitchenette, US$60-70 *palapa* bungalow with fan and kitchenette) offers stylish, comfortable rooms at affordable rates (guests over age 15 only). Units vary in size and layout (some with kitchenettes, some with lofts), but all have fashionable colors, artful stencils, and high-end linens. Rooms open onto a long, leafy central garden with hammocks and low couches, perfect for relaxing day or night. Service is outstanding; purified water, fruit, and baked goods are offered daily.

Hotel Don Diego de la Selva (Av. Tulum s/n, tel. 984/871-2233 or cell. tel. 984/114-9744, www.dtulum.com, US$55 s/d with fan, US$90

s/d with a/c) offers spacious rooms and bungalows with classy understated decor, comfortable beds, and large glass doors looking onto a shady rear garden. There's a large pool, and the hotel restaurant serves good French-Asian-Mexican cuisine; half-board options are available. The only catch is the location, about a kilometer (0.6 mile) south of the plaza. The hotel rents bikes, but most guests find a rental car indispensable. It's very popular with French travelers; wireless Internet and continental breakfast are included.

Set in a leafy garden on the road to Cobá, **Hotel Villas Uolis Nah** (Carr. Tulum-Cobá Km. 0.2, tel. 984/876-4965, www.uolisnah.com, US$63 s/d, US$80 s/d with a/c) has six simple studios with little touches like mosquito-net canopies, mosaic-tile bathrooms, and *palapa*-shaded terraces with hammocks. All units have fully equipped kitchens (even ovens), and one of Tulum's main supermarkets is just down the street. Continental breakfast, bike rental, and wireless Internet are included.

Hotel Nadet (Calle Orión at Calle Polar, 984/871-2114, www.hotelnadet.com, US$80-120 s/d with a/c) offers large, modern, reasonably priced rooms in a central location. While not luxurious, the rooms are quite nice, all with new linens, mini-split air conditioners, and well-equipped kitchenettes. Artful furnishings and decor lend a bit of color and class, and being a block off the main drag makes the hotel, which is operated by a friendly family, convenient but also quiet.

US$100-200

Rooms at **Posada Luna del Sur** (Calle Luna Sur 5 at Av. Tulum, tel. 984/871-2984, www.posadalunadelsur.com, US$99) are compact but tidy and pleasant, with whitewashed walls, comfortable beds (king or two doubles), and small terraces overlooking a leafy garden. Most have kitchenettes, though you may not use it much considering the tasty breakfasts and the many restaurant recommendations of the food-savvy owner-manager. The rooftop lounge is a great evening hangout, and service is excellent. The hotel is for ages 16 and over only.

A short distance from town on the road to the beach, **Teetotum** (Av. Cobá Sur s/n, cell. tel. 984/143-8956, www.teetotumhotel.com, US$125 s/d with a/c) has four sleek minimalist rooms—ceramic basin sinks, low bed stands—and artful decor throughout, including playful oversized murals in the dining room. All rooms have air-conditioning, Wi-Fi, and iPod docks, but no TV or telephone. Guests enjoy free continental breakfast and bike rentals, and a lovely plunge pool and rooftop sun beds, too. There's daily yoga, and various massages and other spa treatments are available on request. The restaurant serves a little of everything, from vegetable dumplings to seafood skewers, with an equally varied (and enticing) drink menu.

Villas Gemini (Calle Andrómeda at Calle Gemini, cell. tel. 984/116-6203, www.villas-geminis.com, US$110/140 one/two bedroom, rate for 4 pax, extra pax US$20) has spacious one- and two-bedroom condos with modern kitchens and private terraces, plus a small swimming pool and 24-hour security—an amazing deal considering they sleep 4-6 people. The owners and staff are attentive and capable, and there's maid service every three days. There's a large supermarket nearby, plus restaurants, bars, and dive shops. The property has cable TV and Wi-Fi, and bikes for rent.

FOOD
Zona Hotelera

◖ **El Tábano** (Carr. Tulum-Punta Allen, 2.2 kilometers/1.4 miles south of junction, cell. tel. 984/134-2706, 8am-11pm daily, US$8-22.50) is Spanish for horsefly, a good sign that this is no ordinary roadside eatery. Rough wood tables on a gravel lot belie a surprisingly nuanced menu, including watermelon gazpacho, pasta-less zucchini lasagna, and fresh fish with red pipian sauce. To drink, try the fresh lemonade or something off the wine list. It can be hot midday, and mosquitoey at dusk—bring repellent.

Fusion Thai is the specialty at **Mezzanine** (Carr. Tulum-Punta Allen, 1.3 kilometers/0.8 mile north of junction, cell. tel. 984/113-1596, www.mezzaninetulum.com, 8am-10pm daily,

US$10-25), one of Tulum's chicest hotels on the beach. Curries—red, green, or pineapple—and fried Thai tofu in peanut sauce are among the dishes served in a fashionable dining area or on a shaded outdoor patio, both with fine sea views. A full bar and cool music make this a place to linger.

La Zebra (Carr. Tulum-Punta Allen, 4.8 kilometers/3 miles south of junction, cell. tel. 984/115-4726, www.lazebratulum.com, 8am-10pm Mon.-Sat., 8am-midnight Sun., US$12-25) has a lovely beachfront patio and *palapa*-roofed dining area; at night, the long entry path is lit by lanterns. The menu is a bit plain—mostly standard fish and chicken dishes—but the Firestone Soup is a treat: seafood soup prepared at your table using a red-hot stone to cook the ingredients. On Sunday there's a barbecue and salsa party starting at 8pm (free dance classes at 6pm).

Posada Margherita (Carr. Tulum-Punta Allen, 2.4 kilometers/1.5 miles south of junction, tel. 984/801-8493, www.posadamargherita.com, 7:30am-10:30am and noon-9pm daily, US$8-30) specializes in gourmet Italian dishes, which are prepared with organic products and homemade pastas and breads. A huge tree-trunk plate of appetizers also is brought to each table (think olives, roasted red peppers, and artichoke hearts)—almost a meal in and of itself. Service is personalized to the point of having no menus—instead, the waiter typically pulls up an extra chair to discuss with you the dishes being prepared that night (ask for prices before ordering—many customers are shocked when the bill arrives). It's busy most nights, so you may have to wait to get a table.

Casa Banana (Carr. Tulum-Punta Allen, 4.7 kilometers/2.9 miles south of junction, tel. 984/877-8512, www.tulumnv.com, 7:30am-9:30pm daily, US$5-15) serves up tasty, well-priced Mexican and Caribbean dishes in a brightly painted patio dining area. Try the *motuleños*, a classic Yucatecan breakfast made with fried eggs, beans, cheese, salsa, and peas all atop a fried tortilla, or the *blaff*, white fish marinated in lime and herbs that will transport you directly to Martinique. Casa Banana is located on the inland side of the road, opposite (and part of) Hotel Nuevo Vida de Ramiro.

In Town

One of the best breakfast places in town, **(Azafrán** (Av. Satélite near Calle Polar, cell. tel. 984/129-6130, www.azafrantulum.com, 8am-3pm daily, US$4-9) serves up superb morning meals made with gourmet products: homemade bagels with prosciutto and Brie, crepes stuffed with an assortment of fresh fruits, *chaya* omelets, and pâté platters with freshly baked bread. Organic coffee is a must, as is the fresh-squeezed orange juice. The only bummer about this place is that there are only six tables—come early to beat the crowd.

Le Bistro (Calle Centauro near Av. Tulum, cell. tel. 984/133-4507, 9am-11pm daily, US$4-15) is a bustling café offering a full range of French delicacies—from freshly baked croissants to duck confit. Tables are set outdoors, either on the front porch or under umbrellas in the back courtyard; neither is very charming, but the food is so good, it's easy to overlook.

Don't let the nautical theme fool you: **La Nave** (Av. Tulum between Calles Beta and Osiris, tel. 984/871-2592, 7am-11pm Mon.-Sat., US$7-14) is more about thin crispy pizza than fish fry. Whether you go all out with a Brie and prosciutto pizza or stick with a classic margherita, you'll leave satisfied. Pasta dishes and hefty appetizers are excellent alternatives.

El Pequeño Buenos Aires (Av. Tulum btwn Calles Orion and Beta, tel. 984/871-2708, 11am-11pm daily, US$6-25) serves excellent cuts of beef, including a *parrillada Argentina,* which comes piled with various cuts, plus chicken and sausage. The menu also includes crepes, a few vegetarian dishes, and lunch specials.

For seafood, don't miss **(Altamar** (Calle Beta near Av. Tulum, cell. tel. 998/282-8299, www.altamartulum.com, 7pm-midnight daily, US$8-15), an upscale restaurant featuring regional dishes like *pan de cazón,* or whole fried fish, prepared using gourmet ingredients and presented with flair. Seating is in an open-air, classy dining room just off Avenida Tulum.

Cooking classes also are offered if you're looking to increase your culinary repertoire.

Cetli (Calle Polar Norte at Calle Orion Norte, cell. tel. 984/108-0681, 5pm-10pm Thurs.-Tues., US$10-20) serves up modern Mexican creations by Chef Claudia Pérez, a Mexico City transplant and a graduate of one of Mexico's top culinary schools. The menu is full of the unique and unexpected, from chicken and *chaya* roll in peanut mole to *agua de pepino con yerba buena* (mint cucumber water). Chef Pérez herself is a delight and often comes out to chat with diners. Reservations can be made via Facebook.

For home-style Mexican cooking, head to **Don Cafeto's** (Av. Tulum btwn Calles Centauro and Orion, tel. 984/871-2207, 7am-11pm daily, US$5-18), serving Mexican staples like mole and enchiladas, plus ceviche plates that are meals unto themselves. On a hot day, try a tall cold *chayagra,* an uplifting blend of pineapple juice, lime juice, cucumber, and *chaya* (similar to spinach).

Taquería El Carboncito (Av. Tulum btwn Calles Acuario and Jupiter; 6pm-2am daily except Tues., US$1-5) serves up hot tacos at plastic tables in the driveway of an auto shop that's closed for the night. That is, it's a great place for a cheap tasty meal, and popular with local families.

Many say Tulum's best seafood is at a low-key outdoor eatery just south of town called **El Camello Junior** (Av. Tulum at Av. Kukulkán, 10:30am-9pm daily except Wed., until 6pm Sun., US$6-12). You won't find any argument here: Ceviche, shrimp cocktail, and made-to-order fish dishes are served super fresh, super tasty, and in generous portions. It's a quick taxi ride or longish walk from town; don't be surprised if you have to wait a few minutes for a table to open up.

Groceries and Bakeries

The Zona Hotelera's largest market, **El Pipazo** (Punta Piedra, 9am-9pm daily) is one room filled with snack food, canned goods, water, liquor, and sunscreen.

For basics and then some, head to the **Super**

San Francisco de Asís (Av. Tulum at road to Cobá, 7am-10pm daily).

Tulum Pueblo has a great local **fruit and vegetable shop** (6am-9pm daily) on Avenida Tulum at Calle Alfa.

A classic Mexican bakery, **Carmen Tulum** (Av. Tulum near Calle Osiris, 6am-11pm daily, US$0.50-1.50) is a bustling shop offering everything from fresh rolls to chocolate-filled *cuernos* (croissants).

INFORMATION AND SERVICES
Tourist Information
A **tourist information kiosk** (no phone, 9am-5pm daily) is located on the central plaza, across from the HSBC bank. The chief attendant is quite knowledgeable, her teenage disciples less so. You often can glean useful information from the stacks of brochures there. The website **www.todotulum.com** also offers good information on current goings-on and offerings in Tulum.

Emergency Services
Tulum's modest local clinic, **Centro de Salud Tulum** (Calle Andrómeda btwn Calles Jupiter and Alfa, tel. 984/871-2050, 24 hours), is equipped to handle minor health problems, but for serious medical issues you should head to Playa del Carmen or Cancún. **Farmacia Similares** (Av. Tulum at Calle Jupiter Sur, tel. 984/871-2736) is open 8am-10pm Monday-Saturday, and 8am-9pm Sunday; it also has a doctor on staff for simple consultations 9am-9pm Monday-Saturday and 9am-3pm Sunday.

The **police** (toll-free tel. 066, 24 hours) share a large station with the fire department, about two kilometers (1.2 miles) from Tulum Pueblo on the road to the Zona Hotelera.

Money
HSBC (Av. Tulum at Calle Alfa next to city hall, 8am-7pm Mon.-Sat.) has a reliable ATM machine and will change foreign cash and AmEx travelers checks.

ScotiaBank (Av. Tulum at Calle Satélite, 8:30am-4pm Mon.-Fri.) has reliable ATMs.

Media and Communications
On the north end of town, **Yaku Ciber** (Av. Satélite near Av. Tulum, 8am-midnight daily except Sat., US$1.25/hour) has flat-screen computers and killer air-conditioning.

Movistar (Av. Tulum at Calle Orion, 9am-10pm daily, US$1/hour) has Skype-enabled computers plus direct-dial international calls (US$0.25-0.40/minute).

In the Zona Hotelera, most hotels offer free Wi-Fi in the reception or restaurant area for guests.

Laundry and Storage
Lava Easy (Av. Tulum btwn Av. Satélite and Calle Centauro, 8am-8pm Mon.-Sat.) charges US$1.25 per kilo (2.2 pounds), with a three-kilo (6.6-pound) minimum.

The **bus terminal** (Av. Tulum btwn Calles Alfa and Jupiter, tel. 984/871-2122, 24 hours) has luggage storage for US$0.50-1.20 per hour depending on the size of the bag.

GETTING THERE
Bus
Tulum's **bus terminal** (Av. Tulum btwn Calles Alfa and Jupiter, tel. 984/871-2122) is at the south end of town, a block from the main plaza.

Combi
Combis are white collective vans that zip between Tulum and Playa del Carmen all day, every day (US$3.50, 1 hour, 24 hours, every 10 minutes 5am-10pm). They leave more frequently than buses and are handier for intermediate stops, like Hidden Worlds, Dos Ojos, Akumal, and Xpu-Há. Flag them down anywhere on Avenida Tulum or Highway 307.

Combis also go to Cobá (US$4.25, 1 hour), stopping at cenotes along the way. They leave at the top of the hour from a stop on Avenida Tulum at Calle Alfa. You can also catch them at the intersection of Highway 307 and the Cobá/Zona Hotelera road.

Tukan Kin (tel. 984/871-3538, www.from-cancunairport.com) operates an **airport shuttle** from Tulum to Cancún airport

TULUM BUS SCHEDULE

Departures from the **bus terminal** (Av. Tulum btwn Calles Alfa and Jupiter, tel. 984/871-2122) include:

DESTINATION	PRICE	DURATION	SCHEDULE
Cancún	US$7-9	2-2.5 hrs	every 15-60 mins midnight-11:30pm
Carrillo Puerto	US$5-6.50	1-1.5 hrs	every 15-60 mins midnight-11:45pm
Chetumal	US$12.50-20	3.5 hrs	every 30-90 mins 12:30am-10:30pm
Chichén Itzá	US$8-12.50	2.5-3 hrs	7:15am, 8:30am, 9am, 2:30pm
Cobá	US$3.50-4	45-60 mins	every 30-60 mins 7:15am-11:15am and 3:30pm-7:15pm
Mahahual	US$13-21.50	3-3.5 hrs	10am and 5:50pm
Mérida	US$20-24.25	3.5-4 hrs	9 departures 1am-9:30pm
Palenque (Chiapas)	US$49-58	10.5-11 hrs	6:25pm, 7:15pm, 10:30pm
Playa del Carmen	US$3.15-5.50	1 hr	every 30-60 mins midnight-11:30pm
Valladolid	US$6-7.50	1.5-2hrs	every 30-90 mins 1:30am-7:30pm

(US$24 adult, US$12 child), with six designated pickup stops around Tulum town and door-to-door service from the Zona Hotelera. Service from the airport to Tulum also is available (US$29 adult, US$14.50 child). The trip takes just under two hours; advance reservations are required.

Car

Highway 307 passes right through the middle of Tulum Pueblo, where it is referred to as Avenida Tulum. Coming south from Cancún or Playa del Carmen, you'll first pass the entrance to Tulum archaeological site, on your left. A kilometer and a half later (1 mile) you'll reach a large intersection, where you can turn left (east) toward the beach and Zona Hotelera, or right (west) toward Cobá. Continuing straight ahead takes you into Tulum Pueblo, then onward to the Costa Maya.

GETTING AROUND
Bicycle

A bike can be very handy, especially for getting to or from the beach, or anywhere along the now-paved road through the Zona Hotelera. **Iguana Bike Shop** (Av. Satélite near Calle Andrómeda, tel. 984/871-2357 or cell. tel.

984/119-0836, www.iguanabike.com, 9am-7pm Mon.-Sat.) rents a variety of bikes, including beach cruisers (US$10 for 24 hours) and mountain bikes (US$13-15 for 24 hours), most in top condition. The owner also leads enjoyable tours to area cenotes and villages (which accounts for the shop sometimes being closed unexpectedly). Rates vary, but include a helmet, front and back lights, lock, and basket, as well as life and accident insurance. English is spoken. Attachable trailer-bikes for children are also available.

Tikul Bike Rental (Av. Tulum at Calle Acuario, cell. tel. 984/114-4657, 8am-10pm daily) rents bikes (US$6/day) and motorscooters (US$29/day), plus snorkel gear (USUS$4.25/day). Helmets are available for scooters only.

Beach Shuttle

There is a local *colectivo* (US$1-1.25) that goes from Tulum town to the arch at the southern end of the Zona Hotelera, and back again, starting at 6am. The last bus leaves the arch at 4pm. Catch it in front of the Palacio Municipal (Calle Osiris near Av. Tulum; departures at the top of the hour) or anywhere along Avenida Tulum or on the road to and along the beach.

The **Weary Traveler Hostel** (Av. Tulum near Calle Acuario, tel. 984/871-2390, www.wearytravelerhostel.com, US$1) operates a beach shuttle that goes north along the Zona Hotelera road. Its final stop is at Playa Maya and Don Cafeto restaurant near the Tulum ruins. Shuttles leave from the hostel at 7am,

9am, and 11:45am, returning at 12:15pm and 5pm.

Bus schedules do change, however, so always confirm the current departures.

Car

A car can be very useful in Tulum, especially in the Zona Hotelera, even if you don't plan on using it every day. Renting a car from the airport in Cancún is the easiest and most affordable option for most travelers, especially if you book online and in advance. In Tulum, agencies include:

- **Hertz** (Hwy. 307 at Carr. Tulum-Cobá, toll-free Mex. tel. 800/709-5000, www.hertz.com, 7am-10pm daily), located next to Super San Francisco supermarket.

- **Thrifty** (Av. Cobá Sur at Calle Sol Ote, tel. 987/869-2957, www.thrifty.com, 8am-2pm and 4pm-6pm daily).

- **Avis** (Av. Cobá Sur at Calle Sol Ote, cell. tel. 984/120-3972, toll-free Mex. tel. 800/288-8888, www.avis.com, 8am-8pm daily).

Taxi

Taxis are plentiful, and fares run about US$2 in town and US$6-10 to get to the Zona Hotelera (depending on where exactly you're going). In the Zona Hotelera, there is a taxi stand in Punta Piedra; rates are roughly the same within the Zona Hotelera or back into Tulum Pueblo. From either area, a ride to Tulum ruins costs about US$4.

Sian Ka'an Biosphere Reserve

Sian Ka'an is Yucatec Mayan for "where the sky is born," and it's not hard to see how the original inhabitants arrived at such a poetic name. The unkempt beaches, blue-green sea, bird-filled wetlands and islets, and humble accommodations are manna for bird-watchers, artists, snorkelers, and kayakers. But most visitors come here for the fishing. Sian Ka'an is one of the best fly-fishing spots in the world, with all three Grand Slam catches: bonefish, tarpon, and permit.

The reserve was created in 1986, designated a UNESCO World Heritage Site in 1987, and expanded in 1994. It now encompasses around 1.3 million acres of coastal and mangrove forests and wetlands, and some 113 kilometers (70 miles) of pristine coral reefs just offshore. A huge variety of flora and fauna thrive in the reserve, including four species of mangrove, many medicinal plants, and about 300 species of birds, including toucans, parrots, frigate birds, herons, and egrets. Monkeys, foxes, crocodiles, and boa constrictors also populate the reserve and are spotted by locals and visitors with some regularity. Manatees and jaguars are the reserve's largest animals but also the most reclusive: You need sharp eyes and a great deal of luck to spot either one. More than 20 Maya ruins have been found in the reserve, though most are unexcavated.

Spending a few days in Sian Ka'an is the best way to really appreciate its beauty and pace. Hotels and tour operators there can arrange fishing, bird-watching, and other tours, all with experienced local guides. But if time is short, a number of tour operators in Tulum offer day trips into the reserve as well.

SIGHTS
Muyil Archaeological Zone
The most accessible Maya site within the Sian Ka'an reserve is **Muyil** (Hwy. 307, 25 kilometers/15.5 miles south of Tulum, 8am-5pm daily, US$3), on the western edge of the park. Also known as Chunyaxché, it is one of the oldest archaeological sites in the Maya world, dating back to 300 BC and occupied continuously through the conquest. It's believed to have been primarily a seaport, perched on a limestone shelf near the edge of Laguna Muyil; it is connected to the Caribbean via a canal system that was constructed by ancient Maya traders and still exists today.

Only a small portion of the city has been excavated, so it makes for a relatively quick visit. There are six main structures ranging from two-meter-high (6.6-foot) platforms to the impressive **Castillo.** At 17 meters (56 feet), it is one of the tallest structures on the peninsula's Caribbean coast. The Castillo is topped with a unique solid round masonry turret from which the waters of the Caribbean Sea can be seen. Unfortunately, climbing to the top is prohibited.

A *sacbé* (raised stone road) runs about a half kilometer (0.3 mile) from the center of the site to the edge of the **Laguna Muyil.** Part of this *sacbé* is on private property, however, so if you want to access the lagoon from the ruins—you also can get to it by car—there is an additional charge of US$3.50 per person. Along the way, there is a lookout tower with views over Sian Ka'an to the Caribbean.

Once you arrive at the water's edge, it's possible to take a **boat tour** (US$45 pp) that crosses both Muyil and Chunyaxché Lagoons, which are connected by a canal that was carved by the ancient Maya in order to reach the ocean. It's a pleasant way to enjoy the water, and you'll also get a view of several otherwise inaccessible ruins along the lagoons' edges and through the mangroves, with the final stop being **Xlapak ruins,** a small site thought to have been a trading post. If arriving by car, look for signs to Muyil Lagoon on Highway 307, just south of the similarly named archaeological site. More thorough tours of this part of Sian Ka'an can be booked in Tulum.

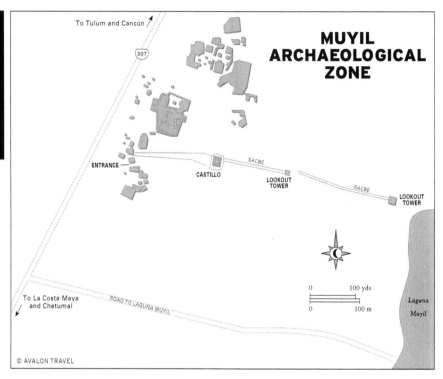

To Tulum and Cancún

307

**MUYIL
ARCHAEOLOGICAL
ZONE**

ENTRANCE

CASTILLO

SACBE

LOOKOUT
TOWER

SACBE

LOOKOUT
TOWER

0   100 yds
0   100 m

To La Costa Maya
and Chetumal

ROAD TO LAGUNA MUYIL

Laguna
Muyil

© AVALON TRAVEL

€ Bahía de la Ascensión

Ascension Bay covers about 20 square kilometers (12.4 square miles), and its shallow flats and tangled mangrove islands teem with bonefish, tarpon, and huge permit—some of the biggest ever caught, in fact. It is a fly fisher's dream come true, and it has been attracting anglers from around the world since the mid-1980s. Don't fly-fish? No worries: The spin fishing is also fantastic, while the offshore reef yields plenty of grouper, barracuda, dorado, tuna, sailfish, and marlin.

SPORTS AND RECREATION
Sportfishing

Sportfishing is world-class in and around Sian Ka'an—it's hard to go wrong in the flats and mangrove islands, or with the Caribbean lapping at its shores. All the hotels listed in this section arrange fishing tours, and most

specialize in it, using their own boats and guides. If you prefer to go with an independent operator, recommended outfits include **Pesca Maya** (7 kilometers/4.3 miles north of Punta Allen, tel. 998/848-2496, toll-free U.S. tel. 888/894-5642, www.pescamaya.com, 8am-7pm daily); the **Palometa Club** (Punta Allen, north of the central plaza, toll-free U.S. tel. 888/824-5420, www.palometaclub.com, 8am-6pm daily); and **Club Grand Slam** (near the entrance to Punta Allen, cell. tel. 984/139-2930, www.grandslamfishinglodge.com).

Weeklong fly-fishing trips range US$2,750-3,750 per person, in shared room and shared boat, depending largely on the style and comforts afforded by the lodge. Most packages include airport transfer, daily guided fishing, meals, and admission to the reserve, but it's always a good idea to confirm this before booking. For private room or private boat, expect to

©LIZA PRADO

a stately pyramid at Muyil archaeological zone, just inside the Sian Ka'an Biosphere Reserve

pay an additional US$100-200 per day; shorter trips are available, but may incur extra transportation costs to and from the airport. Fishing day trips can be arranged through most hotels; rates start at around US$400 for a private full-day tour, including lunch and admission and license fees. Variations like renting gear, adding people, and half-day options can also be arranged.

Bird-Watching

Sian Ka'an is also an excellent place for bird-watching. Trips to Bird Island and other spots afford a look at various species of water birds, including male frigates showing off their big red balloon-like chests in the winter. Tours often combine bird-watching with snorkeling and walking around one or more bay islands. Hotels in Punta Allen and along the coastal road can arrange tours, as can outfits in Tulum. Prices are typically per boat, so don't be shy to approach other travelers in town about forming a group.

In Punta Allen, **Punta Allen Coop** (no phone, 6:30am-2pm daily) is a local cooperative that offers bird-watching tours (US$120-145, 2-3 hours, up to 6 pax); look for their two-story wooden shack along the main road near the entrance to town. Other operators to consider include **CESiaK** (Hwy. 307 just south of the Tulum ruins turnoff, tel. 984/871-2499, www.cesiak.org, 9am-2pm and 4pm-8pm daily); **Community Tours Sian Ka'an** (Tulum, Calle Osiris Sur near Calle Sol Ote, tel. 984/871-2202, www.siankaantours.org, 7am-9pm daily); and, if your budget permits, **Visit Sian Ka'an** (Sian Ka'an Biosphere Reserve, Carr. Tulum-Punta Allen Km. 15.8, cell. tel. 984/141-4245, www.visitsiankaan.com), which offers customized private tours.

Kayaking

The tangled mangrove forests, interconnected lagoons, and scenic bays make Sian Ka'an ideal for kayaking. **CESiaK** (Hwy. 307 just south of the Tulum ruins turnoff, tel. 984/871-2499, www.cesiak.org, 9am-2pm and 4pm-8pm daily) offers kayak tours (US$50, 3 hours) and

SPORT- AND GAME FISHING

Cozumel and the Riviera Maya are well known for trolling and deep-sea fishing, while Ascension Bay and the Costa Maya have terrific fly-fishing. Although you can hook into just about any fish at any time of the year, below is information on the peak and extended seasons for a number of top target species. Those fish not listed—tuna, barracuda, yellowtail, snapper, grouper, and bonefish—are prevalent year-round.

SPORTFISHING

Fish	Peak Season	Extended Season	Description
Sailfish	Mar.–June	Jan.–Sept.	Top target species, with a dramatic dorsal fin and a high-flying fighting style.
Blue Marlin	Apr.–Aug.	Mar.–Sept.	Largest Atlantic billfish, up to 500 pounds locally, but much larger elsewhere.
White Marlin	May–July	Mar.–Aug.	Smaller than the blue marlin, but still challenging.
Wahoo	Nov.–Jan.	June–Feb.	Lightning fast, with torpedo-like shape and distinctive blue stripes.
Dorado	May–July	Feb.–Aug.	Hard fighter with shimmery green, gold, and blue coloration; aka dolphin or mahimahi.

FLAT-WATER FISHING

Fish	Peak Season	Extended Season	Description
Tarpon	Mar.–Aug.	Feb.–Oct.	Big hungry tarpon migrate along the coast in summer months.
Snook	July–Aug.	June–Dec.	Popular trophy fish, grows locally up to 30 pounds.
Permit	Mar.–Sept.	year-round	March and April see schools of permit, with some 20-pound individuals.

rentals for do-it-yourself exploration (US$25/35 s/d, 3 hours). **Community Tours Sian Ka'an** (Tulum, Calle Osiris Sur near Calle Sol Ote, tel. 984/871-2202, www.siankaantours.org, 7am-9pm daily) is another good option.

ACCOMMODATIONS

Punta Allen is the only town on the peninsula and has the most options for lodging, food, tours, and other services. Along the long unpaved road leading there is a smattering of lodges and private homes, amid miles and miles of deserted coastline. **Note:** The town of Punta Allen often switches off the electricity grid at midnight—and hotels outside of town are entirely off the grid—so air-conditioning and TV are not functional unless the establishment has a generator. (Fans work as long as the hotel has solar or wind power.) If you're staying in a room with kitchen facilities, keep the fridge shut as much as possible to conserve the cold.

Toward Punta Allen

Just four kilometers (2.5 miles) from Tulum, **Boca Paila Camps** (tel. 984/871-2499, www. cesiak.org, US$65-80 s/d with shared bathrooms) has spacious "tent cabins"—heavy-duty canvas tents set on platforms—with real beds, tasteful decor, and terraces with views of the Caribbean or lagoon. All share bathrooms with rainwater showers, compost toilets, and 24-hour lighting. The cabins themselves don't have electricity, but candles and battery-powered lamps are provided. There's a restaurant in the main building, where guided kayaking, bird-watching, and fly-fishing tours also can be arranged.

Eight kilometers (5 miles) north of Punta Allen, **C Sol Caribe** (cell. tel. 984/139-3839, www.solcaribe-mexico.com, US$185 s/d, US$175-250 *cabaña*, US$100/40 extra per adult/child all-inclusive) offers modern rooms and *cabañas* set on a breezy palm-tree-laden beach. All feature en suite bathrooms with

© LIZA PRADO

Boca Paila Camps, just inside the Sian Ka'an Biosphere Reserve, offers terrific views from deluxe "tent cabins."

tropical woods, terraces with hammocks, 24-hour electricity (fan only), and gorgeous views of the ocean—a true hidden getaway of the Riviera Maya. There's a full-service restaurant on-site, too.

For more luxury that you'd rightly expect in a remote natural reserve, **Grand Slam Fishing Lodge** (near the entrance to town, cell. tel. 984/139-2930, toll-free U.S. tel. 855/473-5400, www.grandslamfishinglodge.com, US$45-55 s/d with a/c) has gigantic guest rooms in two-story villas, each with one or two king-size beds, fully-stocked minibars, marble bathrooms, and satellite service on large flat-screen TVs, plus 24-hour electricity for air-conditioning and Wi-Fi. The grounds include a tidy beach and aboveground pool, both with drink service, and a spacious restaurant-lounge. Guides and boats are first-rate.

Punta Allen

Casa de Ascensión (near the entrance to town, tel. 984/801-0034, www.casadeascensionhotel.com, US$41-50 s/d with a/c) is a small hotel with three brightly painted rooms, each with quiet air-conditioning, hot-water bathrooms, and Wi-Fi (two also have satellite TV). The owner, a longtime expat, lives on-site and provides attentive service, including breakfast to order in the hotel's 2nd-floor restaurant and recommendations for area tours.

Facing the central plaza, **Posada Sirena** (tel. 984/877-8521, www.casasirena.com, US$38-75 s/d) offers simple Robinson Crusoe-style rooms. Most are quite spacious, sleeping 6-8 people, and all have private bathrooms, fully equipped kitchens, and plenty of screened windows to let in the ocean breeze. Area excursions, including fly-fishing, snorkeling, and bird-watching, can be arranged on-site.

The accommodations at 🄲 **Serenidad Shardon** (road to the lighthouse, cell. tel. 984/107-4155, www.shardon.com, US$8.50-17 pp camping, US$150 s/d, US$200 s/d with kitchen, US$250 two-bedroom apartment for up to 5 guests, US$350 beach house for up to 10 guests) vary from oceanfront *cabañas* to a large beach house; all have basic furnishings

but are clean and well equipped. You also can camp using your own gear, or rent deluxe tents with real beds, electric lighting, and fans; access to hot showers and a full kitchen is included.

A dedicated fishing lodge, **The Palometa Club** (north of the central plaza, toll-free U.S. tel. 888/824-5420, www.palometaclub.com) has just six rooms in a two-story structure facing the beach. Each has tile floors, a private bathroom, and two double beds. Meals are served family-style, with cocktails and snacks (including fresh-made ceviche) available at the club's outdoor bar, après fishing. The Palometa is designed for serious anglers, with a fly-tying study, one-to-one guiding, and an emphasis on landing permits (*palometa* in Spanish, hence the name). Non-anglers are welcome if accompanying a fishing guest. The all-inclusive seven-night/six-day rate is US$3,650 per person (non-anglers US$2,000 per person). Rates are for shared room and boat; for private room, add US$100/night; for private boat, add US$200/day. Shorter packages are available but may include additional airport transfer fees.

FOOD

Punta Allen isn't a foodie's village, but it does have a handful of eateries, all specializing in fresh seafood. A few mini-marts and a tortilleria round things out a bit, especially if you're planning on staying more than a couple of days.

Restaurants

With a gorgeous view of the Caribbean, **Muelle Viejo** (just south of the central plaza, no phone, 11am-10pm Mon.-Sat., US$6-14) serves up fresh seafood dishes and cold beers—perfect for a long lazy lunch.

Taco Loco (just north of the central plaza, no phone, 8am-10pm Mon.-Sat., US$3-8) is a locals' joint with good, cheap eats.

The hotel restaurant at **Casa de Ascensión** (tel. 984/801-0034, www.casadeascensionhotel.com, 8am-10pm daily, US$4-17) offers a wide variety of Mexican dishes, pizza and pasta, and (of course) seafood. Seating is outdoors, under a large *palapa*. It's located two blocks from the beach, near the entrance to town.

Groceries

There are three **mini-marts** in town: on the north end (near the road to the lagoon-side dock), south end (two blocks west of Cuzan Guesthouse), and near the central plaza (one block west). Each sells basic foodstuffs and snacks, though you may have to visit all three to find what you're looking for. If you plan to cook a lot, stock up on supplies in Tulum.

INFORMATION AND SERVICES

Don't expect much in the way of services in Sian Ka'an—if there is something you can't do without, definitely bring it with you. There are **no banking services,** and few of the hotels or tour operators accept credit cards. There is one **Internet café** (9am-9pm Mon.-Fri., 9am-2pm Sat., US$1/hour), located inside a mini-mart near the southwest corner of the central plaza; many hotels have Wi-Fi. Cell phones typically

don't work in Sian Ka'an, but there are **public telephones** in town. Punta Allen also has a modest **medical clinic**—look for it on the main road as you enter town. There is **no laundry,** but most hotels will provide the service.

GETTING THERE

Many of the hotels include airport pickup/drop-off, which is convenient and helps you avoid paying for a week's car rental when you plan on fishing all day. That said, a car is useful if you'd like to do some exploring on your own.

Bus

Public transport to and from Punta Allen is unpredictable at best—build some flexibility into your plans in case of missed (or missing) connections.

A privately run **Tulum-Punta Allen shuttle** (cell. tel. 984/115-5580, US$21, 3 hours) leaves Tulum at 2pm most days. You can catch it at the taxi station on Avenida Tulum between Calles Centauro and Orion, or anywhere along the Zona Hotelera road; advance reservations

the road to Punta Allen, in the heart of Sian Ka'an Biosphere Reserve

The Caste War

On July 18, 1847, a military commander in Valladolid learned of an armed plot to overthrow the government that was being planned by two indigenous men—Miguel Antonio Ay and Cecilio Chí. Ay was arrested and executed. Chí managed to escape punishment and on July 30, 1847, led a small band of armed men into the town of Tepich. Several officials and Euro-Mexican families were killed. The military responded with overwhelming force, burning villages, poisoning wells, and killing scores of people, including many women, children, and elderly. The massacre—and the longstanding oppression of indigenous people at its root—sparked spontaneous uprisings across the peninsula, which quickly developed into a massive, coordinated indigenous rebellion known as the Caste War.

Indigenous troops tore through colonial cities, killing and capturing scores of non-Maya. In some cases, the Maya turned the tables on their former masters, forcing them into slave labor, including building the church in present-day Carrillo Puerto's central plaza. Valladolid was evacuated in 1848 and left abandoned for nearly a year, and by 1849, the peninsula's indigenous people were close to expelling the colonial elite. However, as they were preparing their final assaults on Mérida and Campeche City, the rainy season came early, presenting the Maya soldiers with a bitter choice between victory and (were they to miss the planting season) likely famine. The men turned their backs on a hard-fought and near-certain victory to return to their fields to plant corn.

Mexican troops immediately took advantage of the lull, and the Maya never regained the upper hand. For the next 13 years, captured indigenous soldiers (and increasingly *any* indigenous person) were sold to slave brokers and shipped to Cuba. Many Maya eventually fled into the forests and jungles of southern Quintana Roo. The fighting was rekindled when a wooden cross in the town of Chan Santa Cruz (today, Carrillo Puerto) was said to be channeling the voice of God, urging the Maya to keep fighting. The war ended, however, when troops took control of Chan Santa Cruz in 1901. An official surrender was signed in 1936.

are required. To return, the same shuttle leaves Punta Allen for Tulum at 5am.

You also can get to Punta Allen from Carrillo Puerto, a slightly cheaper but much longer and more taxing trip. State-run *combis* leave from the market in Carrillo Puerto (a block from the main traffic circle) for a bone-jarring four-hour trip down a private road to the small settlement of Playón (US$10, 10am and 3pm daily), where water taxis wait to ferry passengers across the lagoon to Punta Allen (US$2.50 pp, 15 minutes). The *combi* back to Carrillo Puerto leaves Playón at 6am.

Car
To get to Punta Allen by car, head south along the coast through (and past) Tulum's Zona Hotelera. About eight kilometers (5 miles) from the Tulum/Zona Hotelera junction is *el arco* (the arch), marking the reserve boundary where you register and pay a US$4 per person park fee. From there it's 56 kilometers (35 miles) by dirt road to Punta Allen. The road is much improved from years past, and an ordinary car can make it in 2-3 hours. It can be much more difficult after a heavy rain, however. Be sure to fill the tank in Tulum—there is no gas station along the way or in Punta Allen, though some locals sell gas from their homes.

CARRILLO PUERTO
Highway 307 from Tulum to Chetumal passes through Carrillo Puerto, a small city that holds little of interest to most travelers except an opportunity to fill up on gas. Historically, however, it played a central role in the formation of Quintana Roo and the entire peninsula.

History
Founded in 1850, the town of Chan Santa Cruz (present-day Carrillo Puerto) was the center of a pivotal movement during the Caste War. As the

CARRILLO PUERTO BUS SCHEDULE

Departures from the **bus terminal** (Calle 65 near central plaza, tel. 983/834-0815) include:

DESTINATION	PRICE	DURATION	SCHEDULE
Bacalar	US$5.25-7.50	1.5-2 hrs	every 45-60 mins 1:50am-11pm, or take any Chetumal bus
Cancún	US$11.75-16.25	3.5-4 hrs	every 30-90 mins 1:05am-11:45pm
Chetumal	US$6.5-10	2-2.5 hrs	8 departures 8:35am-11:45pm
Mahahual	US$8.25	2 hrs	7pm
Mérida (second-class)	US$18	6 hrs	15 departures 12:30am-8:45pm
Tulum	US$4.75-7.50	1-1.5 hrs	every 30-60 mins 5:30am-11:50pm
Valladolid	US$7	2.5 hrs	11:15pm

Maya lost ground in the war, two indigenous leaders enlisted a ventriloquist to introduce the *Cruz Parlante* (Talking Cross) in Chan Santa Cruz. The cross "spoke" to the battle-weary population, urging them to continue fighting, even issuing tactical orders and predicting victory in the long, bitter conflict. Thousands joined the sect of the cross, calling themselves Cruzob (a Spanish-Maya conflation meaning People of the Holy Cross). Some accounts portray the talking cross as little more than political theater for a simpleminded audience, while others say most Cruzob understood it as a ruse to instill motivation. Some people, of course, believe in the cross's divinity. Whatever the case, it reinvigorated the Maya soldiers, and Chan Santa Cruz remained the last redoubt of organized indigenous resistance, finally submitting to federal troops in 1901. Once residing in Carrillo Puerto's Santuario de la Cruz Parlante, the Talking Cross is today housed in a small sanctuary in the town of Tixcal.

The town's name was changed in 1934 in honor of a former governor of Quintana Roo, much revered by indigenous and working-class people for his progressive reforms, for which he was ultimately assassinated.

Sights

The **Santuario de la Cruz Parlante** (Calle 69 at Calle 60, no phone, irregular hours, free) is a sacred place where the Talking Cross and two smaller ones were originally housed (they now reside in the nearby town of Tixcal). Today, there are several crosses in their place, all dressed in *huipiles,* which is customary in the Yucatán. Shoes and hats must be removed before entering. Be sure to ask permission before snapping any photographs.

Carrillo Puerto's main church, the **Iglesia de Balam Nah** (facing the central plaza, no phone), was reportedly built by white slaves—mostly Spaniards and light-skinned Mexicans—who were captured during the

Caste War. It was constructed in 1858 to house the Talking Cross and its two companion crosses because the original sanctuary had become too small to accommodate its worshippers. Unfortunately, at the end of the Caste War, federal troops used the church as an army storeroom, desecrating it in the eyes of many Maya; this led to the transfer of the Talking Cross to the town of Tixacal.

Despite outward appearances, Maya nationalism is still very much alive, and its adherents are not blind of the sometimes invasive effects of mass tourism. Don't miss the beautifully painted **Central Plaza Mural,** next to the Casa de Cultura, that reads: *La zona Maya no es un museo etnográfico, es un pueblo en marcha* (The Maya region is not an ethnographic museum, it is a people on the move).

Accommodations
Owned and operated by one of the founding families of the city, **Hotel Esquivel** (Calle 63 btwn Calles 66 and 68, tel. 983/834-0344, US$35 s/d with fan, US$42 s/d with a/c, US$55 suite with a/c and kitchenette) offers 37 rooms in four buildings, each with private bathroom and cable TV. The main building has by far the best rooms—gleaming tile floors, simple furnishings, decent beds, and even some with balconies overlooking a pleasant park. The suite is in the large house across the street—once the family home, it's now dark and dilapidated, and desirable only for having a kitchen.

Food
Parrilla Galerías (Calle 65 s/n, tel. 983/834-0313, 5:30pm-midnight daily, US$3-10) opens right onto the central plaza and offers traditional Mexican fare and grilled meats. Come here for the tacos and the *parrillada,* a platter piled high with an assortment of meats, grilled onions, and tortillas.

El Faisán y el Venado (Av. Benito Juárez at Calle 67, tel. 983/834-0043, 6am-10pm daily, US$5-8) is Carrillo Puerto's best-known restaurant, as much for its location and longevity than for any particular noteworthiness of its food. The menu is filled with reliable Yucatecan standards, including 8-10 variations of fish, chicken, and beef, plus soup and other sides.

Information and Services
The **tourist office** (Av. Benito Juárez at Av. Santiago Pacheco Cruz, tel. 983/267-1452) is open 8am-2pm and 6pm-9pm Monday-Friday.

The **Hospital General** (Calle 51 btwn Av. Benito Juárez and Calle 68, tel. 983/834-0092) is open 24 hours daily. Try **Farmacia Similares** (Av. Benito Juárez at Av. Lázaro Cárdenas, tel. 983/834-1407, 8am-10:30pm Mon.-Sat., 9am-10:30pm Sun.) for meds.

The **police department** (central plaza, tel. 983/834-0369, 24 hours) is located in the Palacio Municipal (city hall).

Next to the PEMEX station, **HSBC** (Av. Benito Juárez at Calle 69, 9am-6pm Mon.-Fri., 9am-3pm Sat.) has one 24-hour ATM.

The **post office** (Calle 69 btwn Calles 64 and 66) is open 9am-4pm weekdays. Facing the central plaza, **Balam Nah Internet** (8am-1am daily) charges US$1 per hour.

Getting There
Carrillo Puerto's **bus terminal** (tel. 983/834-0815) is just off the central plaza, with service to Mahahual, Chetumal, Cancún, Mérida, and elsewhere.

If traveling by car, **fill your gas tank** in Carrillo Puerto, especially if you're headed to Mahahual, Xcalak, Xpujil, or Ticul. There are other roadside gas stations ahead (and in Chetumal), but they get less and less reliable—having either no gas or no electricity to pump it—as the stretches of empty highway grow longer and longer.

La Costa Maya

The coastline south of Tulum loops and weaves like the tangled branches of the mangrove trees that blanket much of it. It is a mosaic of savannas, marshes, lagoons, scattered islands, and three huge bays: Bahía de la Ascensión, Bahía del Espiritu Santo, and Bahía de Chetumal. Where it's not covered by mangroves, the shore has sandy beaches and dunes, and just below the turquoise sea is one of the least-impacted sections of the great Mesoamerican Coral Reef. Dozens of Maya archaeological sites have been discovered here, but few excavated, and much remains unknown about pre-Hispanic life here. During the conquest, the snarled coastal forest proved an effective sanctuary for indigenous rebels and refugees fleeing Spanish control, not to mention a haven for pirates, British logwood cutters, and Belizean anglers.

In the 1990s, Quintana Roo officials launched an effort to develop the state's southern coast, which was still extremely isolated despite the breakneck development taking place in and around Cancún. (It has always been a famous fly-fishing area, however.) The first order of business was to construct a huge cruise ship port, which they did in the tiny fishing village of Mahahual. They also needed a catchy name, and came up with "la Costa Maya." The moniker generally applies to the coastal areas south of Tulum, particularly the Sian Ka'an Biosphere Reserve; the towns of Mahahual and Xcalak; Laguna Bacalar; and Chetumal, the state capital and by far the largest city in the area. Few locals use the term, of course.

It's hard not to be a little cynical about cruise liners coming to such a remote area, whose entire population could fit comfortably on a single ship. The town of Mahahual, nearest the port, is utterly transformed when cruise ships arrive, their passengers moseying about Mahahual, beer bottles in hand, the beaches packed with sun worshippers serenaded by the sound of Jet Skis. Then again, it's doubtful the area would have paved roads, power lines, or telephone service if not for the income and demand generated by cruise ships. Driving down the old rutted coastal road to Xcalak (an even smaller town south of Mahahual) used to take a half day or more; today, a two-lane paved road has cut the trip to under an hour. The state government has vowed to control development by limiting hotel size and density, monitoring construction methods, and protecting the mangroves and coral reef. Small ecofriendly bed-and-breakfasts have thrived, not surprisingly, and more and more independent travelers are drawn to the Costa Maya for its quiet isolation and pristine natural beauty.

MAHAHUAL

Mahahual is a place of two faces: cruise ship days, when the town's one road is packed with day-trippers looking to buy T-shirts and throw back a few beers; and non-cruise-ship days, when Mahahual is sleepy and laid-back, and the narrow white-sand beaches are free to walk for miles. Whether you stay here a night or a week, you're likely to see both, which is a good thing. You can be in a major party zone one day, and the next be the only snorkeler in town—all without changing hotels. If you seek long quiet days every day, though, definitely stay outside of town.

Whether or not there is a cruise ship in town, Mahahual is pretty easy to manage. Most of its hotels and services are located on, or just off, Avenida Mahahual (aka El Malecón), the three-kilometer (1.9-mile) pedestrian walkway that runs through town until it meets up with the coastal road heading south, the Carretera Antigua (literally, Old Highway). Just northwest of town, the tiny residential community of Las Casitas (aka Nuevo Mahahual) has additional restaurants, Internet, and laundry services.

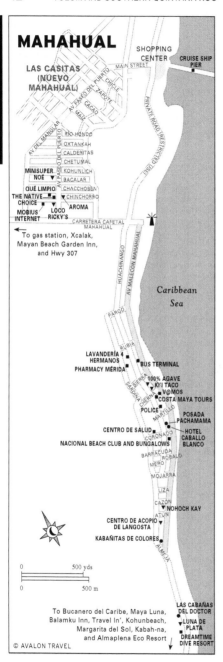

© AVALON TRAVEL

Sports and Recreation
SCUBA DIVING

Mahahual has terrific diving on the coral reef just offshore, with dozens of sites a short boat ride away. It's also one of two jumping-off points for trips to Chinchorro Bank, the largest coral atoll in the Northern Hemisphere. The other departure point is Xcalak, south of Mahahual.

Don't be deterred by the slew of cruise shippers who crowd into **Dreamtime Dive Resort** (Av. Mahahual Km. 2.5, cell. tel. 983/124-0235, www.dreamtimediving.com, 9am-7pm daily)—the shop is an indie operation at heart and sends its students and "regular" guests on separate boats in groups of six divers or fewer. Fun dives cost US$50 for one tank, US$75 for two, and US$20 per day for rental equipment. Open-water, advanced, and other courses are also available.

Bucanero del Caribe (Av. Mahahual Km. 2, cell. tel. 983/120-5306, www.divemahahual. com, 9am-5pm daily) offers personalized service for independent travelers. Dive trips run US$55 for one tank, US$85 for two, including all equipment and a guide.

SNORKELING

You can rent snorkel gear for around US$5-10 a day from the dive shops or from the kiosks that pop up on cruise ship days. Swim or kayak out to the reef for a do-it-yourself experience, or join a guided tour, where you'll likely see more sealife, plus have extra safety and convenience. Mahahual's dive shops all offer guided snorkel trips for US$25-35 per person, including gear and about 90 minutes in the water.

TOURS

The Native Choice (Las Casitas, Av. Paseo del Puerto at Calle Chinchorro, tel. 998/869-3346, www.thenativechoice.com) is a small operation run by David Villagómez and Ivan Cohuo, both born and raised in the small village of Chacchoben and extremely knowledgeable about nearby ruins, Maya history, culture, and belief systems. Tours include visiting the archaeological sites of Chacchoben, Kohunlich,

© LIZA PRADO

a glimpse of Mahahual's beautiful waterfront

or Dzibanche (US$70-90 adult, US$60-85 child), a "Mayan Experience Tour," which includes touring Chacchoben ruins and a visit to a home in Chacchoben village (US$70 adult, US$65 child), plus a kayaking and hiking trip on and around Laguna Bacalar (US$55 adult, US$40 child). The tours are geared toward the cruise ship crowd, but hotel owners warmly recommend the outfit to independent travelers as well.

Accommodations

Many of Mahahual's lodgings, especially the ones with beachfront, are outside of the village itself, along the Carretera Antigua that hugs the coast south of town. The rest are in town, either on the Malecón or a stone's throw away.

IN TOWN

Under US$50: Set on a grassy lot facing the ocean, **Las Cabañas del Doctor** (Av. Mahahual Km. 2, tel. 983/832-2102, www.lascabanasdeldoctor.com, US$6.75 pp camping, US$33-45 *cabaña*, US$45-75 s/d, US$75 s/d with a/c) has

a good range of accommodations: camping on the beach with access to cold-water bathrooms (BYO gear); *cabañas—palapa*-roofed units with tile floors and fans; and hotel rooms, which are a step up in comfort and décor, plus they have private porches.

Kabañitas de Colores (Calle Almeja at Calle Huachinango, cell. tel. 983/137-4095, US$25 s, US$30 d) has a handful of brightly painted clapboard *cabañas*. There's not much to them: a bed, a fan, a bare bulb, a tiny cold-water bathroom. They're clean, though, and there's electricity 24/7. With the beach a stone's throw away, there's not much more you really need.

US$50-100: Posada Pachamama (Calle Huachinango btwn Calles Martillo and Coronado, cell. tel. 983/134-3049, www.posadapachamama.net, US$67-75 s/d with a/c) is a small hotel a block from the beach. Rooms are small but appealingly decorated with modern furnishings and stone-inlaid floors. All have air-conditioning and wireless Internet; the higher-priced rooms include Sky TV. Guests also enjoy complimentary use of the beach club at Los 40 Cañones, just down the street.

With direct access to the beach and a rooftop bar with a spectacular view, **Hotel Caballo Blanco** (Malecón btwn Calles Martillo and Coronado, cell. tel. 983/126-0319, www.hotelelcaballoblanco.com, US$75-108 s/d with a/c) is a great place to land. Rooms are standard issue: modern and comfortable with air-conditioning, flat-screen TVs, and Wi-Fi. The only quirk? Murals of old-world villages in some of the rooms.

Luna de Plata (Av. Mahahual Km. 2, cell. tel. 983/125-3999, www.lunadeplata.info, US$67-92 s/d with a/c) is a restaurant-hotel offering a handful of rooms with tasteful decor. Hot water, quiet air-conditioning, and Wi-Fi cover the basic creature comforts. More expensive rooms have Sky TV, too. Town is an easy walk away, and there's a patch of beach and a dive shop in front.

OUTSIDE OF TOWN

US$50-100: Owned and operated by friendly Canadian expats, **⊂ Balamku Inn on the Beach** (Carr. Antigua Km. 5.7, tel. 983/732-1004, www.balamku.com, US$85 s, US$95 d) offers artfully decorated rooms in a handful of *palapa*-roofed buildings. All run on solar power, wind turbines, and a nonpolluting wastewater system. Full breakfast is included, as is use of the hotel's kayaks, board games, and music and book library. Wi-Fi is available in all the rooms, too.

Kohunbeach (Carr. Antigua Km. 7, cell. tel. 983/700-2820, www.kohunbeach.blogspot.com, US$50 s/d) offers three spacious *cabañas* on the beach. Each has a queen bed, a foldout futon sofa, picture windows, and a mosaic-tile bathroom. All are solar powered. Kayaks and plenty of hammocks are available to guests, too. Continental breakfast is included and delivered to your porch.

Maya Luna (Carr. Antigua Km. 5.6, tel. 983/836-0905, www.hotelmayaluna.com, US$92 s/d) has four modern bungalows with 24-hour solar/wind power, rainwater showers, and *palapa*-shaded porches. Each has a private

rooftop terrace with views of the Caribbean in front and the jungle in back. A hearty and healthy breakfast also is included in the rate. A friendly dog and a handful of cats live—and roam about—the hotel grounds, too.

For a rustic getaway, **Kabah-na** (Carr. Antigua Km. 8.6, cell. tel. 983/116-6919, www.kabahna.com, US$67-75 s/d, US$84-100 s/d with kitchenette) has seven simple *cabañas,* each slightly different, sleeping 3-6 people. All have fans, *palapa* roof, and cold-water showers; those closest to the beach are a bit more polished. There's a decent restaurant on-site, and even a dive and tour guide offering personalized scuba, snorkeling, and other excursions. Guests can make free use of kayaks, snorkel gear, hammocks, and Wi-Fi.

Over US$100: With fully equipped kitchens, the studio apartments at **Margarita del Sol** (Carr. Antigua Km. 7, tel. 555/350-8522, toll-free U.S. tel. 877/473-1934, www.margaritadelsol.com, US$120 studio) are a great option if you want to save a bit on meals. The units themmezzanes are spacious and modern; each has an eating area, a private porch or terrace with an ocean view, and features like wireless Internet and DVD players (plus free access to a decent library of DVDs). Use of kayaks and snorkel gear is also included.

About 20 minutes south of town, **Almaplena Eco Resort and Beach Club** (Carr. Antigua Km. 12.5, cell. tel. 983/137-5070, www.almaplenabeachresort.com, US$140-160 s/d) is a small boutique resort with just eight rooms facing a gorgeous isolated stretch of beach. All have king-size beds, ceiling fans (no air-conditioning), cool stone floors, and tasteful decor. Suites are on the top floor and have private terraces, while standards share a wooden patio with direct access to the beach. Continental breakfast is included, and the on-site restaurant serves fine Italian and Mexican meals. The Italian owners provide friendly and attentive service.

About 21 kilometers (13 miles) north of Mahahual, **Mayan Beach Garden Inn** (Placer town, cell. tel. 983/130-8658, www.mayanbeachgarden.com, US$96-125 s/d, US$125 s/d with kitchenette, US$25 extra for a/c at night) has several rooms and one *cabaña*, all with whitewashed walls and Mexican-style decor, most with ocean views. A hearty breakfast is included in the rate, as are Wi-Fi and the use of kayaks. All-inclusive meal packages are also available. In the high season, there's a three-night minimum.

Food
IN TOWN
With a sand floor, plastic tables, and *palapa* roof, **◖ 100% Agave** (Calle Huachinango btwn Calles Sierra and Cherna, no phone, 8am-11pm Mon.-Sat., US$4-10) won't let you forget that you're at the beach—even if you're a block away. Serving up simple Mexican classics with monster-size drinks, this is a great place to check out the local scene. If it's packed, take a whole roasted chicken to go; it comes with tortillas, potatoes, and grilled onions (US$6).

An open-air eatery and beach club, **Nohoch Kay** (Big Fish in English, Malecón btwn Calles Liza and Cazón, no phone, 8am-7pm Mon.-Tues., 8am-10pm Wed.-Sun., US$5-12) serves up some of the best fish tacos in town. Thick pieces of fish—fried or grilled—are served with small tortillas, onion, cilantro, and plenty of lime. On cruise ship days, it gets overrun with clients, but otherwise it's a laid-back place to get a beachfront meal.

Ki'i Taco (Calle Huachinango at Calle Cherna, no phone, 11am-10pm Mon.-Sat., US$2-6) offers equally good fish tacos without the cruise ship scene. For a treat, order the garlic shrimp tacos.

Luna de Plata (Av. Mahahual Km. 2, cell. tel. 983/125-3999, www.lunadeplata.info, 11:30am-3:30pm and 6pm-midnight daily, US$8-30) serves well-prepared Italian dishes, from thin crispy pizzas to freshly made pasta with shrimp or lobster.

If you're cooking for yourself, consider buying fresh lobster from the local lobster fisherman's co-op, **Centro de Acopio de Langosta** (Calle Huachinango near Calle Almeja, no phone, 7am-7pm daily). At this roadside shack, you can take your pick of lobsters; they

generally sell for US$30 per kilo (2.2 pounds). Fresh conch also is sold here for about US$16 per kilo.

OUTSIDE OF TOWN
A longtime favorite, **Travel In'** (Carr. Antigua Km. 5.8, cell. tel. 983/110-9496, www.travel-in.com.mx, 5:30pm-9pm Tues.-Sat., US$5-20) is a great little restaurant a few kilometers down the coastal road. Pita bread is baked fresh every day—order it as an appetizer with an assortment of homemade dips. Daily seafood specials vary according to the day's catch, plus every Wednesday is tapas night. Open on Mondays from Christmas to Easter.

In Las Casitas, **Aroma** (Las Casitas, Av. Paseo del Puerto s/n, tel. 983/834-5740, 7am-midnight Mon.-Fri., 5pm-midnight Sun., US$4-14) is a cool corner bistro with an open kitchen. An international menu offers respite from standard Mexican fare, with items such as gazpacho, moussaka, and beef medallions in soy balsamic sauce. Wi-Fi is available, too.

Kitty-corner from Aroma, **Loco Ricky's** (Las Casitas, Av. Paseo del Puerto s/n, cell. tel. 983/105-3978, 11am-11pm Tues.-Sun., US$4-14) serves up classic American fare, including burgers, onion rings, and pizza. The bar has a large-screen TV for big games, and the staff makes everyone feel at home (or at least at their hometown sports bar).

For basic groceries, try **Minisuper Noé** (Las Casitas, Av. Paseo del Puerto near Calle Kohunlich, 8am-11pm daily).

Information and Services
Cruise ships have brought considerable modernization to this once-isolated fishing village, but services are still somewhat limited.

EMERGENCY SERVICES
The **Centro de Salud** (Calle Coronado btwn Calles Huachinango and Sardina, no phone, 8am-2:30pm daily, after 5pm emergencies only) offers basic health services. For serious health matters, head to Chetumal.

For meds, try **Pharmacy Mérida** (Calle Sardina btwn Calles Rubia and Sierra, cell.

tel. 983/132-1845, 7am-11pm Mon.-Fri., 9am-11pm Sat.-Sun.), the best-stocked pharmacy in town.

The **police department** (Calle Huachinango near Calle Martillo, toll-free Mex. tel. 066) is open 24 hours.

MONEY
There is no bank in town, but there are a handful of **ATMs,** all along El Malecón. At the time of research, however, none were affiliated with local banks, so withdrawal charges were hefty. Another option is to go to the gas station outside of town, where there's an **HSBC ATM** (though it often runs out of cash); alternatively, consider bringing enough money to get you through your stay.

MEDIA AND COMMUNICATIONS
In Mahahual proper, head to **V@mos** (Calle Cherna between El Malecón at Calle Huachinango, cell. tel. 983/106-4647, 9am-3pm and 7pm-9pm daily, US$1.75 per hour) for Internet service. If there's a long wait and you've got a car, head to Las Casitas, where **Mobius Internet** (9am-9pm Mon.-Sat.) charges US$3 per hour and offers international telephone service, too (US$0.30-0.60/minute calls to the United States and Europe). Most hotels and some restaurants offer wireless Internet as well.

LAUNDRY
Lavandería 4 Hermanos (Calle Huachinango near Calle Rubia, 7am-8pm daily) offers same-day laundry service for US$1.25 per kilo (2.2 pounds).

In Las Casitas, try **Qué Limpio** (Calle Chacchoben 24, 8am-6pm Mon.-Sat.), which charges US$1.25 per kilo (2.2 pounds). Service takes a day or two.

VOLUNTEER WORK
Global Vision International (www.gvi.co.uk) operates a popular volunteer-for-pay program just north of Mahahual, in partnership with Amigos de Sian Ka'an, a local nonprofit. GVI "expeditions," as they are called, last 4-12 weeks. Fees are reasonable considering how much diving is involved (including open-water scuba certification, if needed): US$3,052 for 4weeks, US$5,772 for 12 weeks, including room, board, and equipment, but no airfare. Advance registration is required, as the center is not designed to handle walk-ins. GVI also has programs in Sian Ka'an Biosphere Reserve as well as at the private inland reserve El Eden.

Getting There and Around
Just south of the grubby roadside town of Limones, a good paved road with signs to Mahahual breaks off Highway 307 and cuts through 58 kilometers (36 miles) of coastal forest and wetlands tangled with mangroves. It's a scenic stretch, whether in a car or on a bus, along which you can see occasionally egrets, herons, and other water birds.

Mahahual proper is very walkable—in fact, the main road that runs through town, El Malecón, is a three-kilometer (1.9-mile) pedestrian walkway. If you're staying outside of town, a car certainly comes in handy, but plenty of people manage without; dive shops and tour operators typically offer hotel pickup, and there are cabs and a local bus.

BICYCLE
Bike rentals are offered at **Costa Maya Tours** (Calle Cherna between El Malecón at Calle Huachinango, cell. tel. 983/106-4647, 9am-3pm and 7pm-9pm daily) for US$2.50 per hour, US$7.50 per half day, and US$12.50 per day. **Nacional Beach Club and Bungalows** (Calle Huachinango near Calle Coronado, tel. 983/834-5719) also rents bikes at similar rates.

BUS
Mahahual's bus terminal is a modest affair—an open-air lot near the entrance of town—but daily first-class service makes coming and going a breeze. Buses to Cancún (US$23, 5 hours) leave at 8:30am and 1pm daily, stopping at Carrillo Puerto (US$8.25, 2 hours), Tulum (US$14.50, 3 hours), Playa del Carmen (US$17, 3.5 hours), and Puerto Morelos (US$19, 4 hours) along the way. To Chetumal

(US$10, 2.5 hours) and Laguna Bacalar (US$7, 1.5 hours), buses depart at 7:30am and 6:30pm daily. All buses stop in Limones (US$7, 1.5 hours). The ticket booth is open a short time before and after scheduled departures only.

Note: Buses entering Mahahual stop in Las Casitas before arriving at the bus terminal; be sure you get off at the latter if you're headed to the beach or any of the hotels.

There also is occasional bus service to Xcalak (Mon.-Sat., US$3); buses pass through the center around 9am and drive down the coastal road, passing most of the hotels there before joining the main paved road into Xcalak. The bus heading back to town from Xcalak passes the outlying hotels around 3:30pm.

CAR AND TAXI

There is a PEMEX gas station (24 hours) on the main road to Mahahual, just east of the turn-off to Xcalak. It occasionally runs out of gas, so definitely fill your tank in Carrillo Puerto or Chetumal on your way here.

Note: There's often a military checkpoint set up just west of the turnoff to Xcalak, where officials conduct searches for illicit drugs and other contraband. As long as you or your passengers don't have anything illegal in the car, the longest you should be delayed is a couple of minutes.

Cabs abound in this town, especially on cruise ship days. In general, rates run US$1.25 per kilometer (0.6 mile).

AIRPORT

Mahahual has a small airport just outside of town. Well, it's more like a well-maintained airstrip with a nice shelter. At the time of research, it was only used by private or chartered planes.

XCALAK

The tiny fishing village of Xcalak lies just a short distance from the channel that marks the Mexico-Belize border, and a blessed long way from anything else. The town started out as a military outpost and didn't get its first real hotel until 1988. Villagers had to wait another decade to get a paved road; before that, the only

way in or out of town was by boat or via 55 kilometers (34 miles) of rutted beach tracks. Electrical lines were installed in 2004 but only in the village proper, so many outlying areas (including most of the better hotels) still rely on solar and wind power, as well as generators. The town has no bank, no public phones, and no gas station. That is to say: perfect!

The area doesn't have much beach but makes up for it with world-class fly-fishing, great snorkeling and diving, and a healthy coral reef and lagoon. A growing contingent of expats, mostly American and Canadian, have built homes here, some for personal use, others for rent, others as small hotels. Large-scale tourism may be inevitable but still seems a long way off, and Xcalak remains a small and wonderfully laid-back place, perfect for those looking for some honest-to-goodness isolation.

Sights

PARQUE NACIONAL ARRECIFES DE XCALAK

Xcalak Reef National Park was established at the end of 2003, affording protection to the coastal ecosystem as well as Xcalak's nascent tourist economy. The park spans nearly 18,000 hectares (44,479 acres), from the Belize border to well north of town, and includes the reef—and everything else down to 100 meters (328 feet)—as well as the shoreline and numerous inland lagoons.

The main coral reef lies just 90-180 meters (100-200 yards) from shore, and the water is less than 1.5 meters (5 feet) deep almost the whole way out. Many snorkelers prefer the coral heads even closer to shore, which have plenty to see and less swell than the main reef. The shallow waters keep boat traffic to a minimum, and anglers are good about steering clear of snorkelers (you should still stay alert at all times, however).

Divers and snorkelers also can explore the reef at 20 or so official sites and many more unofficial ones. Most are a short distance from town, and shops typically return to port between tanks. **La Poza** is one of the more distinctive dives, drifting through a trench where

© LIZA PRADO

Kayaking is a great way to enjoy the Costa Maya.

hundreds, sometimes thousands, of tarpon congregate, varying in size from one-meter (3-foot) "juveniles" to two-meter (7-foot) behemoths.

A fee of US$5 per day technically applies to all divers and snorkelers (and kayakers and anglers) in the Parque Nacional Arrecifes de Xcalak; dive shops typically add it to their rates, while most hotels have a stack of wristband permits to sell to guests who want to snorkel right from shore.

🞄 BANCO CHINCHORRO

Chinchorro Bank is by some measurements the largest coral atoll in the Northern Hemisphere and a paradise for divers and snorkelers alike. About 48 kilometers (30 miles) northeast from Xcalak, Chinchorro is a marine reserve and is known for its spectacular coral formations, massive sponges, and abundant sealife. Scores of ships have foundered on the shallow reefs through the years, but (contrary to innumerable misreports) the wrecks cannot be dived. Not only are they protected as historical sites, but most are on

the eastern side of the atoll, where the surf and currents are too strong for recreational diving. The famous **40 Cannons wreck,** in about three meters (10 feet) of water on the atoll's northwest side, is good for snorkeling but not diving, and thanks to looters there are far fewer than 40 cannons there. There are small government and fishermen's huts on one of the three cays, Cayo Centro; as of 2010, tourists are finally permitted to stay overnight, which means spectacular multiday diving and snorkeling opportunities.

Sports and Recreation
SCUBA DIVING AND SNORKELING

XTC Dive Center (north end of town, across bridge, no phone, www.xtcdivecenter.com, 9am-5pm daily) is a full-service dive shop that specializes in trips to Chinchorro Bank; its acronym officially stands for "Xcalak to Chinchorro," though the nearby ecstasy-inducing dives surely figured into the name. Trips to Chinchorro are US$199 per person for two tanks or US$149 per person for snorkelers, including lunch, drinks, and a hike on Cayo Centro, the main cay; multiday trips also are available. To get to Chinchorro, it's a 1.5- to 2-hour boat ride, which can be pretty punishing depending on conditions. Groups typically set out around 7am and return to port around 4:30 or 5pm. Dive shops usually require at least five divers or six snorkelers (or a combination of the two) and may not go for days at a time if the weather is bad (summer months are best). Closer to home, reef dives cost US$60 for one tank, US$90 for two; equipment costs extra. Snorkel tours run US$30-65 per person depending on how long and far you go; five-hour trips include jaunts into Chetumal Bay and Bird Island, which can be fascinating, especially in January and February when the birds are most plentiful. A 10 percent tax applies to most rates.

Costa de Cocos (3 kilometers/1.9 miles north of town, no phone, www.costadecocos.com) also offers diving, as does Casa Carolina (2.5 kilometers/1.6 miles north of town, U.S. tel. 610/616-3862, www.casacarolina.net). Prices at all three shops are comparable.

SPORTFISHING

Xcalak also boasts world-class sportfishing, with huge saltwater and brackish flats where hooking into the grand slam of fly-fishing—tarpon, bonefish, and permit—is by no means impossible. Add a snook, and you've got a super slam. Oceanside, tarpon and barracuda abound, in addition to grouper, snapper, and others. Costa de Cocos (3 kilometers/1.9 miles north of town, no phone, www.costadecocos.com) is the area's oldest fishing resort, with highly experienced guides and numerous magazine write-ups. Three- to seven-night packages include transfer to and from the airport, lodging, meals, open bar, and, of course, nonstop fly-fishing (US$1,830-4,105 s, US$1,420-3,095 d). Hotel Tierra Maya (2.1 kilometers/1.3 miles north of town, toll-free U.S. tel. 800/216-1902, www.tierramaya.net) also offers fly-fishing packages for 3-7 nights (US$1,370-3,605 s, US$770-2,099 d), though

they don't include all the perks that the Costa de Cocos packages do. The dive shops, as well as most hotels, also can arrange guided fishing tours.

Accommodations

Xcalak's most appealing accommodations are on the beach road heading north out of town. Few places accept credit cards on-site, but many have payment systems on their websites.

UNDER US$50

Xcalak Caribe (south of the lighthouse, no phone, www.xcalakcaribe.com, US$37.50 s/d) has large clean rooms, each with ceiling fan and private bathroom, just steps from the beach. The expat owners are friendly and attentive, and the restaurant here, specializing in Mediterranean-style seafood, is outstanding.

Right at the entrance of town, Cabañas Tío Bon (cell. tel. 983/836-6954, US$25 s/d) is a basic but reasonably clean option. Three wood cabins alongside the owner's home—you share a front gate—have tiny private bathrooms, fan, and 24-hour electricity. The plywood interior and lack of hot water will prevent any confusion between Uncle Bon's and the Westin.

US$50-100

Hotel Tierra Maya (2.1 kilometers/1.3 miles north of town, toll-free U.S. tel. 800/216-1902, www.tierramaya.net, US$90-100 s/d, US$150 apartment) is a pleasant hotel with ample rooms decorated with simple furnishings and colorful Mexican rugs. All have private terraces or balconies with views of the Caribbean. Continental breakfast is included in the rate and served in the hotel's excellent beachfront restaurant. Fly-fishing and dive packages are also available.

Xcalak's first hotel and oldest fishing and diving lodge, Costa de Cocos (3 kilometers/1.9 miles north of town, no phone, www.costadecocos.com, US$78 s, US$90 d) eschews fluff and formality for a jocular laid-back atmosphere that's perfectly suited to its clientele.

Simple wood-paneled *cabañas* are comfortable enough, with tile floors and hot water, and surround a well-kept sandy lot. Travelers looking for "charming" won't find it here, and that seems to be just how it's preferred. Continental breakfast is included.

US$100-150

It's hard not to feel at home at **❰ Sin Duda** (8 kilometers/5 miles north of town, U.S. tel. 415/868-9925, www.sindudavillas.com, US$84 s/d, US$110 studio, US$120 apartment), a gem of hotel with beautifully decorated rooms featuring Mexican folk art and breathtaking views. Evening often brings cocktail hour, when guests can join the friendly American hosts for margaritas in the cozy lounge that doubles as a common kitchen and library. A healthy continental breakfast, brought to your room, is included in the rate.

Four cheerful units with fully equipped kitchenettes make **Casa Carolina** (2.5 kilometers/1.6 miles north of town, U.S. tel. 610/616-3862, www.casacarolina.net, US$100 s/d) a great choice for indie travelers. Add ocean views from private balconies and a wide beach with palm trees, and it's a classic beach vacation. Co-owner Bob Villier is an experienced NAUI dive instructor and offers personalized certification classes plus diving and snorkeling trips. Continental breakfast, with divine homemade muffins, is included.

OVER US$150

Playa Sonrisa (6.9 kilometers/4.3 miles north of town, no phone, www.playasonrisa.com, US$135-175 s/d, US$175-225 suite) is a clothing-optional resort on a palm-tree-laden stretch of beach. Units are clean and comfortable, though they lack the charm that you'd expect for the rate. What you mostly pay for is the freedom to enjoy the Caribbean in the buff. A continental breakfast buffet is included in the rate, as is Wi-Fi. Geared at naturist couples, the hotel welcomes naturist families during the low season only. Day

passes are available to naturist couples, too (10am-sunset, US$20 pp).

Food

The **❰ Leaky Palapa** (2 blocks north of the lighthouse, no phone, www.leakypalaparestaurant.com, hourly seatings 5:30pm-8:30pm Thurs.-Sun., Nov.-May only, US$16-23) is a gourmet restaurant with boho flair and a menu that changes according to the day's catch and market offerings. It is invariably delicious, though, with such dishes as homemade ravioli with *huitlacoche* (corn fungus), lobster, and squash flower cream as well as snapper on a bed of plantain mash with green coconut salsa. Reservations are required and only cash is accepted.

Locally run **Restaurant Toby** (center of town, across from volleyball court, cell. tel. 983/107-5426, 11am-10pm Mon.-Sat., US$5-10) is a popular seafood restaurant serving up, among other tasty dishes, heaping plates of ceviche, coconut shrimp, and fish soup. It's a friendly, low-key place perfect for a beer and a good meal after a day of diving or relaxing on the beach. Wi-Fi is available, too.

Xcalak Caribe (no phone, www.xcalak-caribe.com, 11am-3pm and 5:30pm-10pm Tues.-Sun., US$5-20) serves seaside standards like ceviche and garlic grilled fish, as well as Mediterranean specialties, like paella and Gallego-style octopus. Cocktails are served from a bar artfully fashioned from the hull of an old fishing boat. Restaurant options are slim in Xcalak, but the tasty dishes, friendly service, and casual atmosphere would make this a popular eatery anywhere. Look for the *palapa*-roofed building just south of the lighthouse, facing the beach.

The Maya Grill (Hotel Tierra Maya, 2.1 kilometers/1.3 miles north of town, toll-free U.S. tel. 800/216-1902, www.tierramaya.net, 5pm-9pm daily, US$12-22) is a beachfront hotel restaurant offering fresh ingredients in its Mexican-inspired meals. As expected, seafood is the focus, but chicken and meat dishes edge their way onto the menu, too. Dinners are pricey but hearty.

The restaurant at **Costa de Cocos** (3 kilometers/1.9 miles north of town, no phone, www.costadecocos.com, 7am-10pm daily, US$5-28) serves up burgers, steak, pizza, and all manner of tall tales—though with fishing as good as it is, many just happen to be true. The service is seriously lacking, but the schedule, reservations policy (none required), and full bar make it a reliable option.

A popular culinary event is the weekly chicken barbecue at **Maya Campground** (north end of town, across bridge, no phone, US$5), held every Wednesday afternoon. Come early to get the best of the bird, which is served with coleslaw and beans.

If you are cooking for yourself, a **grocery truck** passes through town and down the coastal road several times per week—ask at your hotel for the current schedule. It comes stocked with eggs, yogurt, grains, basic produce, fresh meats, and canned food. You also can buy a broom or two. In town, there are a handful of small **mini-marts** selling basic canned and dried foods. Most are open daily 9am-9pm.

Information and Services
Xcalak has **no bank, ATM, or currency-exchange office,** and only a few places take credit cards—plan accordingly!

There's a basic **health clinic** (no phone, 8am-noon and 2pm-6pm Mon.-Fri.) two blocks from the soccer field, near the entrance of town.

Most hotels have Wi-Fi; in a pinch many hotel owners will let you use their computers to send a quick email. For more time on the net, **San Jordy** (center of town, hours vary, US$4/hour) is a reliable Internet café. To make an international or domestic call, head to **Telecomm/Telégrafos** (near The Leaky Palapa, 9am-3pm Mon.-Fri.).

Getting There and Around
Bus service is somewhat erratic in Xcalak.

Theoretically, buses bound for Chetumal (with stops in Mahahual and Limones) leave twice daily, typically around 5am and 2pm (US$7, 4-5 hours), but it's not unusual for one or both departures to be delayed or canceled. Upon arrival, your hotel may send a car to pick you up; otherwise a taxi from town is about US$10.

Most travelers come in a rental car, which certainly simplifies life here. The closest gas station is on the main road to Mahahual, near the turnoff for Xcalak. However, it occasionally runs out of gas, so you should fill up on Highway 307 as well—Carrillo Puerto is a good spot. In a pinch, a few Xcalak families sell gas from barrels in their front yards; ask your hotel owner for help locating them.

If your budget permits, there also is a well-maintained airstrip approximately 2 kilometers (1.2 miles) west of town. Despite rumors that commercial flights will begin using it regularly, at the time of research, it was only used sporadically by private or chartered planes.

CHACCHOBEN ARCHAEOLOGICAL ZONE
Chacchoben (8am-5pm daily, US$4) got its name from archaeologists who, after uncovering no inscription indicating what the city's original residents called it, named it after the Maya village to which the land pertained. The meaning of that name is also lost, even to local villagers, though the accepted translation is Place of Red Corn. The area may have been settled as early as 1000 BC, and most of the building activity probably took place AD 200-700, the Classic period.

Visiting the Ruins
Entering the site, a short path leads first to **Temple 24,** a squat pyramid that is the primary structure of a small enclosed area called **Plaza B.** Across that plaza—and the larger Gran Plaza beyond it—is a massive

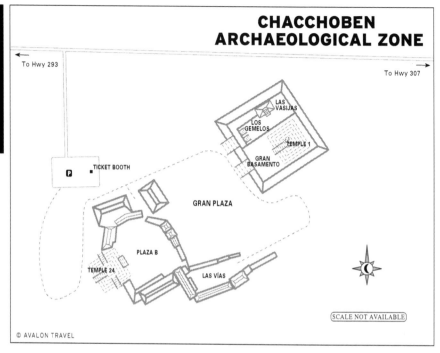

**CHACCHOBEN
ARCHAEOLOGICAL ZONE**

To Hwy 293

To Hwy 307

LAS VASIJAS

LOS GEMELOS

TEMPLE 1

GRAN BASAMENTO

TICKET BOOTH

GRAN PLAZA

PLAZA B

TEMPLE 24

LAS VÍAS

SCALE NOT AVAILABLE

© AVALON TRAVEL

raised platform, the **Gran Basamento,** with the site's largest pyramid, **Temple 1,** atop it; this pyramid is believed to have served astronomical and religious purposes. Also on the platform, two smaller structures, dubbed **Las Vasijas** and **Los Gemelos,** were likely used for ceremonial functions. The site has some well-preserved stucco and paint, and for that reason none of the pyramids can be climbed. Though it can get crowded when there's a cruise ship at Mahahual, Chacchoben has an appealingly remote feel, nestled in the forest with towering mahogany and banyan trees, and paths dotted with bromeliads.

Practicalities

Chacchoben is located about 70 kilometers (43 miles) north of Mahahual and 4 kilometers (2.5 miles) west of Limones. By **car,** take Highway 307 and turn west at the sign to Chacchoben ruins and like-named town, about 3 kilometers (1.9 miles) down a well-paved road. Alternatively, take a **bus** to Limones and then a **cab** (US$5) to the ruins.

Laguna Bacalar

Almost 50 kilometers (31 miles) long, Laguna Bacalar is the second-largest lake in Mexico and certainly among the most beautiful. Well, it's not technically a lake: A series of waterways do eventually lead to the ocean, making Bacalar a lagoon, but it is fed by natural springs, making the water on the western shore, where the hotels and town are, 100 percent *agua dulce* (fresh water).

The Maya name for the lagoon translates as Lake of Seven Colors. It is an apt description, as you will see on any sunny day. The lagoon's sandy bottom and crystalline water turn shallow areas a brilliant turquoise, which fades to deep blue in the center. If you didn't know better, you'd think it was the Caribbean.

The hub of the Laguna Bacalar region is the town of Bacalar. Located on the west side of

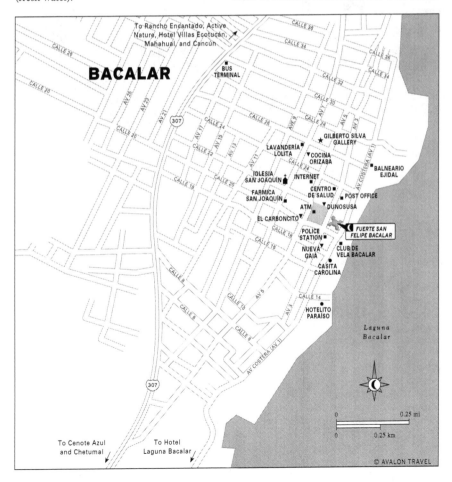

To Rancho Encantado, Active Nature, Hotel Villas Ecotucán, Mahahual, and Cancún

BACALAR

BUS TERMINAL

GILBERTO SILVA GALLERY

LAVANDERÍA LOLITA

COCINA ORIZABA

BALNEARIO EJIDAL

IGLESIA SAN JOAQUÍN

INTERNET

FARMCIA SAN JOAQUÍN

CENTRO DE SALUD

POST OFFICE

ATM

DUNOSUSA

EL CARBONCITO

POLICE STATION

FUERTE SAN FELIPE BACALAR

NUEVA GAIA

CLUB DE VELA BACALAR

CASITA CAROLINA

HOTELITO PARAÍSO

Laguna Bacalar

To Cenote Azul and Chetumal

To Hotel Laguna Bacalar

0   0.25 mi

0   0.25 km

© AVALON TRAVEL

© LIZA PRADO

Fuerte San Felipe Bacalar is a restored fort with an excellent museum inside.

the lake, it won't win any prizes for charm, but it does have a terrific museum, one of the best hotels around, a handful of decent restaurants, and, of course, gorgeous views of the lagoon.

SIGHTS AND EVENTS
◖ Fuerte San Felipe Bacalar

The mid-18th-century **Fuerte San Felipe Bacalar** (central plaza, no phone, Av. 3 at Calle 20, 9am-7pm Tues.-Thurs. and Sun., 8am-8pm Fri.-Sat., US$5) was built by the Spanish for protection against English pirates and Maya that regularly raided the area. In fact, attacks proved so frequent—and successful—that the fort was captured in 1858 by Maya during the Caste War. It was not returned to Mexican officials until 1901. Today, the star-shaped stone edifice has been restored to its former glory: drawbridge, cannons, moat, and all. The fort also houses the excellent **Museo del Fuerte de San Felipe Bacalar,** a modern museum with exhibits on the history of the area, including details on the pirates who regularly attacked these shores.

Cenote Azul

As good or better than Laguna Bacalar for swimming, **Cenote Azul** (Hwy. 307 Km. 15) is two kilometers (1.2 miles) south of town. It's the widest cenote in Mexico, some 300 meters (984 feet) across at its widest, and 150 meters (492 feet) deep, with crystalline blue water. A rope stretches clear across, so even less-conditioned swimmers can make it to the far side. A large, breezy **restaurant** (tel. 983/834-2038, 7:30am-8pm daily, US$6-16) has the only entrance to the cenote, and doesn't charge admission if you order something.

Gilberto Silva Gallery

Gilberto Silva, an accomplished sculptor of Maya art, has a small **gallery and workshop** (Calle 26 btwn Calles 5 and 7, tel. 983/834-2657, hours vary) where some of his works are displayed and sold. Most are intricately carved limestone pieces, which are then cast in clay. Notably, his works have been displayed at the Museum of Natural History in New York City.

Fiesta de San Joaquín

Every July, the town of Bacalar celebrates San Joaquín, its patron saint. For nine consecutive days, different neighborhoods host festive celebrations, each trying to outdo the other for the year's best party. Visitors are welcome and should definitely join the fun—expect plenty of food, music, dancing, and performances of all sorts. Cockfights also are popular, and a three-day **hydroplane race** usually follows the festivities in early August.

SPORTS AND RECREATION
Ecotours

A friendly German couple founded **Active Nature** (Hotel Villas Ecotucán, Hwy. 307 Km. 27.3, cell. tel. 983/120-5742, www.active-naturebacalar.com) after fate and car trouble cut short their planned tour of the Americas and left them in lovely Laguna Bacalar. Tour options include kayaking through mangrove channels to hidden lagoons and freshwater beaches, sunset and moonlight outrigger canoe rides, biking to a great curassow breeding reserve and research center, and morning bird-watching walks. Prices range US$12.50-50 per person, including gear and often lunch and water; children under 10 are free, under 14 half off. Tours begin at Villas Ecotucán, whose guests get a 10 percent discount. Multiday kayak and paddle sailing tours are also available.

Páay bej Tours (Av. 5 btwn Calles 24 and 26, tel. 983/839-0830, www.bacalar-tours-paaybej.com) also offers kayaking tours of the lagoon and mangrove channels (US$37.50 pp), bike tours around the village with a visit to Fuerte San Felipe (US$17 pp), and guided tours of Chacchoben and other Maya ruins (US$37.50 pp, including transport and entrance fees). You can also rent bikes here (US$1.75/hour, US$8.50/day).

Kayaking

The **Club de Vela Bacalar** (Av. Costera at Calle 20, tel. 983/834-2478, 9am-6pm Mon.-Sat.) rents kayaks for US$8.50 per hour (single or double). **Active Nature** (Hotel Villas Ecotucán,

Hwy. 307 Km. 27.3, cell. tel. 983/120-5742, www.activenaturebacalar.com) organizes kayaking tours, as does the local tour company, **Páay bej Tours** (Av. 5 btwn Calles 24 and 26, tel. 983/839-0830, www.bacalar-tours-paaybej.com).

Swimming

The **Balneario Ejidal de Bacalar** (Av. Costera near Calle 26, no phone, 7am-7pm, US$0.75) is a public swimming area complete with *palapas* for rent (US$3/day), bathrooms, and a restaurant (9am-7pm, US$3-10). Located just 250 meters (0.2 mile) from the central plaza, it's a convenient and inexpensive place to enjoy the water.

The pier at the **Club de Vela Bacalar** (Av. Costera at Calle 20, tel. 983/834-2478, 9am-6pm Mon.-Sat.) is one of the best places to swim in town, with a long footbridge leading to a swimming dock, where the water is crystal clear and deep. Order something from the restaurant and stay as long as you want.

Other good swimming spots on Laguna Bacalar include **Rancho Encantado** (2 kilometers/1.2 miles north of town, tel. 983/839-7900, www.encantado.com) and **Hotel Laguna Bacalar** (Blvd. Costero 479, tel. 983/834-2206, www.hotellagunabacalar.com); plan on ordering something from the hotel restaurant to be able to use the waterfront.

Yoga and Spa

Nueva Gaia (Av. 3 near Calle 18, tel. 983/834-2963, www.gaia-maya.com, 8am-4pm Tues.-Sun.) offers various types of massage, from relaxation massage (US$48, 60 minutes) to hot stone massages (US$66, 80 minutes), in its holistic center near the central plaza.

ACCOMMODATIONS
In Town

One of the area's most charming and convenient accommodations, ⦅ **Casita Carolina** (Av. Costera btwn Calles 16 and 18, tel. 983/834-2334, www.casitacarolina.com, US$37.50-58.50 s/d, US$30-50 s/d with shared kitchen) offers lagoon-front units that open onto a large

© LIZA PRADO

Find utter tranquility at little-visited Laguna Bacalar.

grassy garden. Units are either stand-alone or occupy a converted home, but all have a private bathroom, a fan, and a homey feel. The friendly American owner lives on-site and is a wealth of information on area sights.

Hotelito Paraíso (Av. Costera at Calle 14, tel. 983/834-2787, www.hotelitoelparaiso.un-lugar.com, US$54 s/d with a/c) has 14 stark hotel rooms, with minifridge, cable TV, and Wi-Fi. All open onto a large grassy area that runs to the lakeshore; there's a *palapa* shade, plenty of chairs, and even a grill. Kayaks also are available for rent for US$4.50 per hour.

Outside of Town

Villas Ecotucán (Hwy. 307 Km. 27.3, cell. tel. 983/120-5743, www.villasecotucan.info, US$62.50-71 s/d) has five *palapa*-roofed *cabañas* and one suite, each spacious and simple, with a veranda to enjoy the view of the lake and surrounding tropical forest. Rates include two adults and two kids under 12, full breakfast for all, and use of the kayaks,

dock, and trails. Guided excursions—bike, kayak, sailboat, and on foot—also are available.

Rancho Encantado (Hwy. 307 Km. 24, tel. 983/839-7900, toll-free U.S. tel. 877/229-2046, www.encantado.com, US$120-142 s/d with fan, US$127-221 with a/c, breakfast included) has spacious *palapa*-roofed casitas and modern suites, both featuring Mexican tile floors, good beds, and views of either the lush garden or the lagoon. The prettiest spot here, however, is a pier that leads to a shady dock strung with hammocks—it's perfect for swimming and relaxing. Guests can receive massages and body treatments in a small kiosk built over the lake; a hot tub is nearby. The only downer here is the persistent hum of traffic from nearby Highway 307.

Built on a bluff just south of town, **Hotel Laguna Bacalar** (Blvd. Costero 479, tel. 983/834-2205, www.hotellagunabacalar.com, US$89 s/d with a/c) has spacious rooms, most with a balcony and dramatic views of the lagoon. The decor, once seriously kitschy, has been toned down to a bit of shell art. Stairs zig-zag down to the water, where a pier, ladder, and a diving board make swimming in the lagoon easy. There's a small pool, too. Wi-Fi also is available for a nominal daily fee.

FOOD

For good cheap eats, **Cocina Orizaba** (Av. 7 btwn Calles 24 and 26, tel. 983/834-2069, 8am-6pm daily, US$3.50-10) serves a variety of classic Mexican dishes. The daily *comida corrida* (lunch special) includes an entrée, main dish, and drink.

On the main plaza, **Restaurante y Pizzería Bertilla** (Av. 5 at Calle 20, cell. tel. 983/123-4567, 4pm-11pm Tues.-Sun., US$6-15) specializes in homemade pasta and pizza. Some traditional Mexican dishes are available, too.

El Carboncito (central plaza, Av. 5 near Calle 20, 7pm-11pm daily, US$2.50-6) is a popular *puesto* (food stand) that serves up grilled favorites like hot dogs, hamburgers, and tacos. If you want your meal to go, let the cook know it's *"para llevar."*

Groceries

Dunosusa (Calle 22 btwn Avs. 3 and 5, 7:30am-9pm Mon.-Sat., 8:30am-8pm Sun.) is a well-stocked supermarket on the central plaza.

INFORMATION AND SERVICES
Tourist Information

Bacalar does not have a tourist information office yet, but **www.bacalarmosaico.com** is a bilingual website offering useful information on the area's sights, activities, and businesses.

Emergency Services

The **Centro de Salud** (Av. 3 btwn Calles 22 and 24, tel. 983/834-2756, 24 hours) offers basic medical care; for serious matters, head to Chetumal. For meds, try **Farmacia San Joaquín** (Av. 7 btwn Calles 20 and 22, no phone, 8am-3pm and 6pm-9pm daily). The **police station** (Calle 20 near Av. 3, toll-free Mex. tel. 066, 24 hours) is located across from the Fuerte San Felipe Bacalar.

BACALAR BUS SCHEDULE

Departures from the **bus terminal** (Hwy. 307 near Calle 30, no phone) are almost all *de paso* (mid-route service), which means there's often a limited availability of seats. Destinations include:

DESTINATION	PRICE	DURATION	SCHEDULE
Cancún	US$17.50-23	5-6 hours	every 30-60 mins 5:45am-11:30pm
Carrillo Puerto	US$5.25-7.75	1.5-2 hours	take Cancún bus
Chetumal	US$2.50-3.50	50 mins	every 30-60 mins 6:05am-11:55pm
Mahahual	US$6.50	2 hours	6:15am and 8:15pm
Playa del Carmen	US$13.50-18.25	4-4.5 hours	take Cancún bus
Tulum	US$11-12	2.5-3 hours	take Cancún bus

Money

There is no bank in town, but there is a **Banorte ATM** on the west side of the central plaza. If you need other money services or the ATM has run out of cash, the closest bank is in Chetumal.

Media and Communications

The **post office** (Av. 3 near Calle 24, 8am-4:30pm Mon.-Fri., 8am-noon Sat.) is just east of the Fuerte San Felipe Bacalar. For email try the **no name Internet** (Av. 5 near Calle 24, 9am-10pm daily, US$1/hour), operated out of the living room of a private home. For telephone calls, your best bet is to use the **public phones** on the central plaza; Ladatel telephone cards can be purchased at the supermarket and at most corner stores.

Laundry

Lavandería Lolita (Av. 7 btwn Calles 24 and 26, tel. 983/834-2069, 9am-8pm daily) offers same-day service for US$1 per kilo (2.2 pounds). Pickup and delivery are available.

GETTING THERE AND AROUND

You can easily walk to all the sites of interest in Bacalar, with the exception of Cenote Azul. A taxi there from town costs around US$3; cabs typically wait for passengers around the central plaza and on Avenida 7 in front of Iglesia San Joaquín.

Bus

Bacalar's modest **bus terminal** (Hwy. 307 near Calle 30) is on the highway, about a 20-minute walk from the central plaza. The buses are almost exclusively *de paso* (midroute) service, which means there's often limited availability (i.e., as soon as you know your schedule, buy your ticket).

Combi

Combis and *taxi colectivos* (US$2-3, every 30 minutes) run between Bacalar and Chetumal daily. You can catch either in front of Iglesia San Joaquín (Calle 22 near Av. 7), one block up from the central plaza.

Chetumal

Chetumal is the capital of Quintana Roo and the gateway to Central America. It's not the prettiest of towns, and most travelers just pass through on their way to or from Belize or southern Campeche. However, Chetumal's modern Maya museum is one of the best you'll find in the region (albeit with few original pieces) and is well worth a visit. And if you're dying to see the Guatemalan ruins of Tikal, a shuttle from Chetumal can get you there in eight hours (cutting through Belize) and back again just as fast; a 90-minute boat ride also will take you to San Pedro, Belize, for a quick overnighter. The area around Chetumal is worth exploring, too, whether the bayside town of Calderitas or the intriguing and little-visited Maya ruins of Kohunlich, Dzibanché, Kinichná, and Oxtankah. North of town is Laguna

Bacalar, a beautiful multicolored lake with great swimming and kayaking.

SIGHTS
Museo de la Cultura Maya

One of the best museums in the region, the **Maya Culture Museum** (Av. de los Héroes at Calle Cristóbal Colón, tel. 983/832-6838, 9am-7pm Tues.-Sun., US$5) extends over three levels—the upper represents the world of gods, the middle the world of humans, and the lower Xibalba, the underworld. Each floor has impressive, well-designed exhibits describing Maya spiritual beliefs, agricultural practices, astronomy and counting, and more, all in English and Spanish. In fact, the only thing lacking is original artifacts. (The copies, however, are quite good.) The exhibition area past the ticket booth usually has good temporary

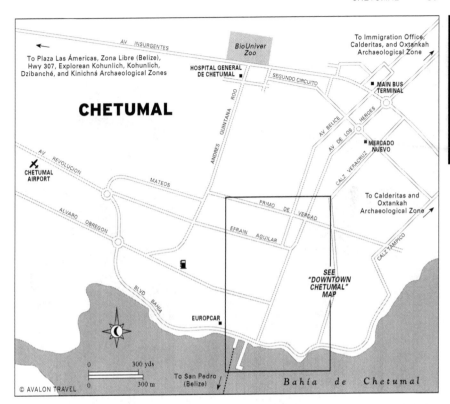

art shows, plus a cinema that hosts free screenings of independent films.

Monumento al Mestizo

Across from the Museo de la Cultura Maya is the **Monumento al Mestizo** (Av. de los Héroes s/n), a striking sculpture symbolizing the creation of a new race—the mestizo—through the union of the Spanish shipwrecked sailor Gonzalo Guerrero and Zazil Há, a Maya woman. Hernán Cortés offered to take Guerrero back to Spain, but Guerrero chose to stay in the Americas, wedding Zazil Há in a Maya marriage ritual. Note that the Maya symbol for the number zero as well as the cycle of life, the snail shell, provides the framework for the entire work of art.

Museo de la Ciudad

The **city museum** (Calle Héroes de Chapultepec btwn Avs. Juárez and de los Héroes, tel. 983/832-1350, 9am-7pm Tues.-Sat., 9am-2pm Sun., US$1) is small and well organized, and describes the political, economic, and cultural history of Chetumal, spanning the period from its founding in 1898 to the present day. Signage is in Spanish only.

El Malecón

Running six kilometers (3.7 miles) on the Boulevard Bahía, this breezy promenade makes for a fine bayfront stroll. Along it you'll find cafés, monuments, a lighthouse, government buildings, and, hopefully, a cooling breeze. Of particular note are two impressive **murals** found within the **Palacio Legislativo** (end of Av. Reforma, 9am-10pm Mon.-Fri.), a shell-shaped building that houses the State Congress. Created by local artist Elio Carmichael, one

TULUM AND QUINTANA ROO

© LIZA PRADO

The Museo de la Cultura Maya in Chetumal has fascinating displays on Maya sculpture, writing, mathematics, astronomy, and more.

mural outlines the state's history—from the creation of man to the devastating effects of Hurricane Janet in 1955—while the other depicts the law of the cosmos. Both are located in the reception area and are free for public viewing.

Maqueta Payo Obispo

The **Maqueta Payo Obispo** (Calle 22 de Enero near Av. Reforma, 9am-7pm Tues.-Sun., free) is a scale model of Chetumal as it looked in the 1930s, with brightly colored clapboard houses, grassy lots, and plenty of palm trees. It's a reproduction of a model made by longtime resident Luis Reinhardt McLiberty. Look for it in a glass-enclosed building across the street from the Palacio Legislativo, though glare on sunny days can make it hard to see the exhibit. A small history museum of the city also is on-site; signage is in Spanish only.

Trolley Tours

For a breezy overview of Chetumal's attractions, consider taking **Bule Buzz** (cell. tel. 983/120-5223, US$8 adult, US$5 child), a guided trolley tour of the city. Sites visited include the murals in the Palacio Legislativo, the sculptures along Boulevard Bahía, the Maqueta Payo Obispo, and the Museo de la Cultura Maya. The trolley leaves from the Monumento al Mestizo at noon and 3pm Tuesday-Saturday and 11am Sunday; admission to the Museo de la Cultura Maya also is included.

ENTERTAINMENT AND SHOPPING
Sunday on El Malecón

Every Sunday at 6pm, locals gather at the **Esplanada de la Bandera** (southern end of Av. de los Héroes) to enjoy city-sponsored events, typically performances by the municipal band or local musicians and singers. The events are

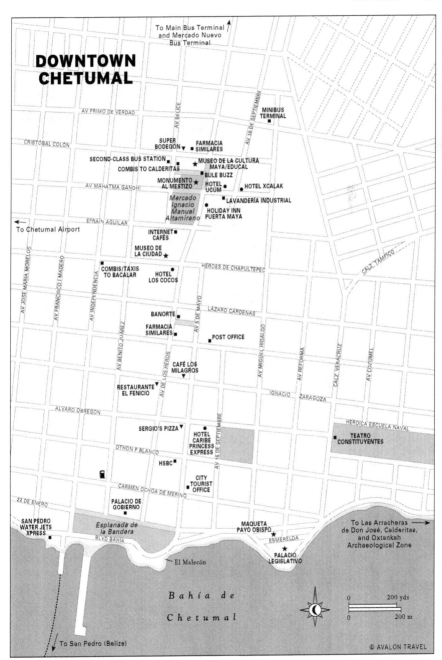

DOWNTOWN CHETUMAL

To Main Bus Terminal and Mercado Nuevo Bus Terminal

AV PRIMO DE VERDAD

AV BELICE

AV 16 DE SEPTIEMBRE

MINIBUS TERMINAL

CRISTÓBAL COLÓN

SUPER BODEGON

FARMACIA SIMILARES

SECOND-CLASS BUS STATION

MUSEO DE LA CULTURA MAYA/EDUCAL

COMBIS TO CALDERITAS

BULE BUZZ

MONUMENTO AL MESTIZO

AV MAHATMA GANDHI

HOTEL UCUM

HOTEL XCALAK

Mercado Ignacio Manuel Altamirano

LAVANDERÍA INDUSTRIAL

EFRAÍN AGUILAR

HOLIDAY INN PUERTA MAYA

To Chetumal Airport

INTERNET CAFÉS

MUSEO DE LA CIUDAD

AV JOSÉ MARIA MORELOS

AV FRANCISCO I MADERO

AV INDEPENDENCIA

COMBIS/TAXIS TO BACALAR

HOTEL LOS COCOS

HEROES DE CHAPULTEPEC

CALZ. TAMPICO

AV BENITO JUÁREZ

BANORTE

AV 5 DE MAYO

LÁZARO CÁRDENAS

FARMACIA SIMILARES

POST OFFICE

AV MIGUEL HIDALGO

AV REFORMA

CALZ VERACRUZ

AV COZUMEL

AV DE LOS HEROES

CAFÉ LOS MILAGROS

RESTAURANTE EL FENICIO

IGNACIO ZARAGOZA

ALVARO OBREGON

HEROICA ESCUELA NAVAL

SERGIO'S PIZZA

HOTEL CARIBE PRINCESS EXPRESS

AV 16 DE SEPTIEMBRE

TEATRO CONSTITUYENTES

OTHON P. BLANCO

HSBC

CITY TOURIST OFFICE

CARMEN OCHOA DE MERINO

22 DE ENERO

PALACIO DE GOBIERNO

SAN PEDRO WATER JETS XPRESS

Esplanada de la Bandera

BLVD BAHIA

MAQUETA PAYO OBISPO

ESMERELDA

To Las Arracheras de Don José, Calderitas, and Oxtankah Archaeological Zone

PALACIO LEGISLATIVO

El Malecón

Bahía de Chetumal

0   200 yds
0   200 m

To San Pedro (Belize)

© AVALON TRAVEL

free and family friendly, with vendors selling drinks and street food.

Cinema

If you're hankering to watch the latest Hollywood film, head to **Cinépolis** (Plaza Las Américas, Av. Insurgentes s/n, tel. 983/837-6043, www.cinepolis.com, US$3-5), an 11-screen theater where most films are in English with Spanish subtitles.

Shopping

Educal (Av. de los Héroes at Calle Cristóbal Colón, cell. tel. 983/129-2832, www.educal.com.mx, 9am-7pm Tues.-Sat., 9am-2pm Sun.) is a good bookstore located inside the Museo de la Cultura Maya.

Mercado Ignacio Manuel Altamirano (Efraín Aguilar btwn Avs. Belice and de los Héroes, 8am-4pm daily) is a two-story building mostly selling everyday items, from clothing to kitchenware. For travelers, it's a good place to buy a pair of flip-flops, a travel clock, or kitschy souvenirs.

Plaza Las Américas (Av. Insurgentes s/n, 9am-10pm daily) is a classic shopping mall with clothing and shoe boutiques, a Chedraui supermarket, a megaplex movie theater, and all the typical amenities, like ATMs, food court, and public bathrooms.

The **Zona Libre** (Corozal Duty Free Zone, 9am-7pm daily) is an area jam-packed with stores selling products from around the world. It's located in Belize, and visitors can enter and leave the area without passports or paying taxes on their purchases, mostly household and personal items. (There's a US$1 entrance fee, however.)

ACCOMMODATIONS

Chetumal's status as the state capital and its location on the Belize border make it a busy town, and reservations are recommended.

Under US$50

Hotel Xcalak (Av. 16 de Septiembre at Av. Mahatma Gandhi, cell. tel. 983/129-1708, www.hotelxcalak.com.mx, US$38 s/d with

a/c) is the best budget deal in town: modern rooms with tasteful decor, strong but quiet air-conditioning, SKY TV, and wireless Internet. The hotel restaurant also provides room service (though you've got to order in person). The hotel is located one block from the Museo de la Cultura Maya.

Next door, the aqua-colored **Hotel Ucúm** (Av. Mahatma Gandhi btwn Avs. 5 de Mayo and 16 de Septiembre, tel. 983/832-0711, www.hotelucumchetumal.com, US$18 s/d with fan, US$23 s/d with fan and cable TV, US$32 s/d with a/c and cable TV) has aging but clean rooms. Beds are hit or miss, unfortunately, and some rooms can be downright stuffy (ask for one on the top floor for the best breeze). There's a decent pool on-site with a separate wading area for kids. There's also a secure parking lot.

US$50-100

Hotel Caribe Princess Express (Av. Alvaro Obregón btwn Avs. 5 de Mayo and 16 de Septiembre, tel. 983/832-0900, toll-free Mex. tel. 866/337-7342, US$42 s with a/c, US$50 d with a/c, US$64 suite with a/c) has comfortable nondescript rooms with decent beds, cable TV, and powerful air-conditioning. There's Wi-Fi in the lobby and a self-serve breakfast (i.e., toast, cereal, fruits) every day. Ask for a room facing the interior of the building; the karaoke bar in front blasts music—and keeps the windows rattling—until late.

Hotel Los Cocos (Av. de los Héroes at Calle Héroes de Chapultepec, tel. 983/835-0430, toll-free Mex. tel. 800/719-5840, www.hotelloscocos.com.mx, US$76-152 s/d with a/c) has three categories of rooms, all pleasant with updated furnishings and modern amenities. The more expensive ones have flat-screen TVs, quiet air conditioning, and more stylish decor. They all open onto a lush garden, which has a small inviting pool area. The on-site restaurant is great for breakfast.

Over US$100

Holiday Inn Chetumal-Puerta Maya (Av. de los Héroes near Av. Mahatma Gandhi, tel. 983/835-0400, toll-free U.S. tel. 888/465-4329, www.holidayinn.com, US$100-132 s/d with a/c) is the nicest hotel in town, with marble floors, wood-beam ceilings, and high-end amenities. There's a gym on-site, as well as a well-maintained pool, which is surrounded by a tropical garden. Kids also stay for free. Be sure to check the website for reservations—there often are terrific deals.

Outside of Chetumal

On the road to the like-named ruins, **C Explorean Kohunlich** (tel. 555/201-8350, toll-free Mex. tel. 800/504-5000, toll-free U.S. tel. 800/343-7821, www.theexplorean.com, US$320-640 suite), is a luxurious resort with 40 deluxe suites set on 30 hectares (74 acres) of tropical forest. Each has gleaming stone floors, high *palapa* ceilings, elegant furnishings, and privacy walls for sunbathing. Two suites also have plunge pools. The main building houses a fine restaurant (7:30am-10:30pm daily, US$12-24, open to nonguests), a full-service spa, and a lap pool that overlooks the jungle (you can see the ruins at Kohunlich from here). One excursion per day—rappelling in the jungle, kayaking through a crocodile reserve, or mountain biking through forgotten forests—is included. Transportation to and from Chetumal's airport also is thrown in.

FOOD

Restaurante El Fenicio (Av. de los Héroes at Calle Zaragoza, tel. 983/832-0026, 24 hours, US$4-10) is a local favorite, not only because it's open around-the-clock but also because of its tasty, reliable meals. Be sure to try the "make your own taco" dish, a platter stacked with chicken, chorizo, beef, and melted cheese, served with tortillas and all the fixings.

A buzzing little place, **C Café Los Milagros** (Calle Ignacio Zaragoza near Av. 5 de Mayo, tel. 983/832-4433, 7:30am-9pm Mon.-Sat., 7:30am-1pm Sun., US$3-7) serves up strong coffee drinks and especially good breakfasts. The best seating is outdoors—snag a table where you can, as it can get crowded fast.

Located on the Malecón, **Las Arracheras**

de Don José (Blvd. Bahía at Calle Josefa Ortiz de Dominguez, tel. 983/832-8895, 6pm-1am daily, US$4-10) serves some of the best tacos in town. Try the *tacos de arrachera* (broiled skirt steak marinated in lemon and spices), which can only be improved when downed with a cold beer.

Sergio's Pizza (Av. 5 de Mayo at Av. Alvaro Obregón, tel. 983/832-0491, 7am-midnight daily, US$5-17) serves much more than pizza in its dimly lit dining room. The extensive menu covers the gamut of Italian and Mexican dishes—from meat lasagna to *molletes rancheros*. Meals are hearty, making it popular with families.

Super Bodegón (Calle Cristóbal Colón btwn Avs. Belice and de los Héroes, 5am-9pm Mon.-Sat., 5am-3pm Sun.) is a grocery store with an impressive selection of fresh fruits and veggies. Canned goods, dry foods, and basic toiletries are also sold.

INFORMATION AND SERVICES

Tourist Information

Near the waterfront, the **city tourist office** (Av. 5 de Mayo at Carmen Ochoa de Merino, tel. 983/835-0860, 8:30am-4:30pm Mon.-Fri.) has a decent selection of brochures and maps. There also is a **tourist information booth** in the main bus terminal (Av. Insurgentes at Av. de los Héroes, 9am-8pm daily).

Emergency Services

About two kilometers (1.2 miles) from the center of town, **Hospital General de Chetumal** (Avs. Andrés Quintana Roo at Juan José Isiordia, tel. 983/832-8194, 24 hours) is the city's main hospital. For meds, try **Farmacia Similares** (Av. de los Héroes near Calle Plutarco Elias, tel. 983/833-2232, 8am-9pm daily) or its **sister store** (Calle Cristóbal Colón btwn Avs. Belice and de los Héroes, tel. 983/833-2331), which is open 24 hours. The **police** can be reached by dialing toll-free 066.

Money

HSBC (Av. Othon Blanco btwn Av. 5 de Mayo

and Av. de los Héroes, 8am-7pm Mon.-Sat.) and **Banorte** (Av. de los Héroes btwn Lázaro Cárdenas and Plutarco Elias, 9am-4pm Mon.-Fri.) are both conveniently located downtown. There also is an ATM at the **bus station.**

Media and Communications

The **post office** (Av. Plutarco Elias Calles btwn Avs. 5 de Mayo and 16 de Septiembre, 8am-4pm Mon.-Fri., 9am-1pm Sat.) is just a block from the main drag. For Internet access, there is a string of **Internet cafés** across from the Mercado Ignacio Manuel Altamirano (Efraín Aguilar btwn Avs. Belice and de los Héroes); most charge US$1 per hour and are open 7am-midnight daily. At the main bus station, **Cafeteria El Kiosko** (8am-8pm daily) has a row of computers (US$1.50/hour) and telephone service (US$0.50/minute worldwide).

Immigration

The **immigration office** (Calzada del Centenario 582, tel. 983/832-6353, 9am-1pm Mon.-Fri.) is located on the road to Calderitas; signage is hard to spot, so keep your eyes peeled for the building.

Laundry and Storage

Though catering primarily to hotels and restaurants, **Lavandería Industrial** (Av. Mahatma Ghandi near Av. 16 de Septiembre, no phone, 8am-8pm daily) charges US$1.25 per kilo (2.2 pounds) and also takes small loads. There is no signage, so listen for the huge dryers and look for huge piles of tablecloths—it's surprisingly easy to miss.

Conveniently located in the main bus station, **Lockers, Revistas y Novedades Laudy** (Av. Insurgentes at Av. de los Héroes, 8am-8pm daily) stores bags for US$0.50 per hour.

GETTING THERE AND AROUND

Chetumal is a relatively large city, but the parts most travelers are interested in are all within easy walking distance—mostly along Avenida de los Héroes and El Malecón. The exception is the main bus terminal and Mercado Nuevo, both of which are 10-12 grubby blocks from the center. A cab to either terminal, or anywhere around downtown, costs US$2-3.

Air

The **Chetumal Airport** (CTM, tel. 983/832-6625) receives only a few flights each day. Airlines serving it include **Interjet** (toll-free Mex. tel. 800/011-2345, toll-free U.S. tel. 866/285-9525, www.interjet.com.mx) and the air taxi service **Avioquintana** (tel. 998/734-1975, www.avioquintana.com).

Bus

All first-class buses leave from the **main bus terminal** (Av. Insurgentes at Av. de los Héroes, tel. 983/832-5110, ext. 2404), though most second-class buses stop here on the way in or out of town.

The **second-class bus station** (Avs. Belice and Cristóbal Colón, tel. 983/832-0639) is located just west of the Museo de la Cultura Maya; tickets for first-class buses also can be purchased here if you want to buy your tickets in advance but don't want to make the trek to the main terminal.

Two other terminals—the **Minibus terminal** (Av. Primo de Verdad at Av. Miguel Hidalgo, no phone) and **Mercado Nuevo** (Av. de los Héroes and Circuito Segundo, no phone)—have service to Bacalar, the Zona Libre, and to Belize.

Combi

Combis and *taxi colectivos* (US$1.50-2, every 30 minutes) run between Chetumal and Bacalar daily. You can catch either on Avenida Independencia at Calle Héroes de Chapultepec.

Car

The highways in this area are now all paved and well maintained. Car rental agencies in town include **Continental Rent-a-Car** (Holiday Inn, Av. de los Héroes near Av. Mahatma Ghandi, tel. 983/832-2411, www.continentalcar.com.mx, 8am-8pm daily) and **Europcar** (Chetumal

CHETUMAL BUS SCHEDULE

Departures from Chetumal's **main bus terminal** (Av. Insurgentes at Av. de los Héroes, tel. 983/832-7806) are for first-class service, though some second-class buses stop here as well (tickets for either service can be purchased downtown, in the **second-class bus terminal** (Av. Belice at Av. Cristóbal Colón). Destinations from the main bus terminal include:

DESTINATION	PRICE	DURATION	SCHEDULE
Bacalar	US$2.50-3.50	50 mins	every 15-60 mins 5:30am-11:45pm
Campeche	US$28.25	6.5 hours	noon
Cancún	US$17-25.50	5.5-6.5 hours	every 30-90 mins 4am-12:30am
Mahahual	US$10	2.5 hours	5am and 7:30pm, or take Xcalak bus (second-class only)
Mérida	US$30.50	5.5-6 hours	7:30am, 1:30pm, 5pm, and 11:30pm
Palenque	US$23-33	6.5-7.5 hours	9:45pm, 9:50pm, 11pm
Playa del Carmen	US$16-21	4.5-5 hours	take any Cancún bus
Tulum	US$12.50-15	3.5-4 hours	take any Cancún bus
Xcalak	US$10	4-5 hours	6am and 4:30pm, or 5:40am and 4:10pm in Mercado Nuevo terminal
Xpujil	US$5.75-9	1.5-2 hours	every 45-90 mins 6:30am-11:59pm

Buses for **Corozal** (US$4.50, 1 hour), **Orangewalk** (US$6, 2 hours), and **Belize City** (US$9.50, 3 hours) leave the **Mercado Nuevo** (Av. de los Héroes at Circuito Segundo, no phone) 18 times daily 4:30am-6:30pm. Some pass the main ADO terminal en route.

Buses to the **Zona Libre** (US$2, 30 minutes) leave the **Minibus terminal** (Av. Primo de Verdad at Av. Miguel Hidalgo, no phone) every 15 minutes 6:30am-8pm.

Noor Hotel, Blvd. Bahía at Ave. José Maria, tel. 983/833-9959, www.europcar.com, 8am-8pm daily).

Taxi

Taxis can be flagged down easily in downtown Chetumal. Few are metered, so be sure to agree on a price before you set off toward your destination.

Water Taxi

San Pedro Water Jets Xpress (Blvd. Bahía near Av. Independencia, tel. 983/833-3201, www.sanpedrowatertaxi.com) offers direct service to Ambergris Caye, Belize. Trips take 90 minutes and leave at 3:30pm daily, returning the following day at 8am (US$40 one-way, US$75 round-trip). Transfers to Caye Caulker and Belize City are also available.

Around Chetumal

The area around Chetumal has a number of worthwhile attractions, all the better because so few travelers linger here.

CALDERITAS

Located just seven kilometers (4 miles) north of Chetumal, Calderitas is a bayside town known for its **seafood restaurants** (8am-6pm daily, US$4-10)—most along the waterfront across from the main plaza—and its **public beaches.** During the week it's a mellow scene, but on weekends locals descend upon the town for a day of R&R and some revelry, too.

Boat rides can be arranged at many of the bayside establishments to explore **Chetumal Bay** (US$150, up to 8 people) in search of manatees, which were once abundant in these waters, or to visit **Isla Tamalcab** (US$40, up to 8 people), an uninhabited island with white-sand beaches and good snorkeling, and home to spider monkeys and *tepescuintles* (pacas in English).

If you want to stay overnight, the best place in town is **Yax Há Resort** (Av. Yucatán 415, tel. 983/834-4127, www.yaxha-resort.com, US$8.50 pp camping, US$20-30 per RV, US$42-58 s/d with fan, US$125 s/d with a/c and kitchenette). Located on the waterfront, it offers everything from camp- and RV sites to

Spanish missionaries often had their churches built alongside or atop ancient Maya ruins, like this chapel and archway found at the Oxtankah ruins near Chetumal.

© LIZA PRADO

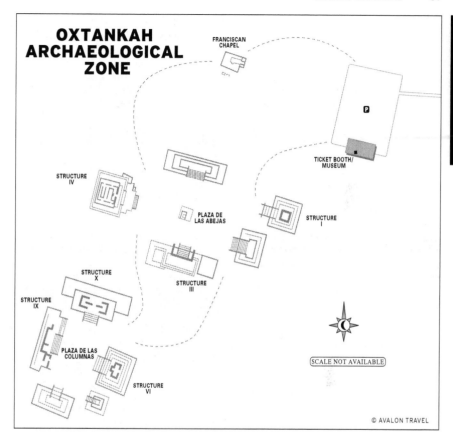

bungalows. The bungalows themselves range from simple one-room units with a minifridge and microwave to two-bedroom units with fully equipped kitchens; all have porches with chairs that overlook the bay. There also is a pool on-site and a restaurant, too.

Getting There

Calderitas is a quick bus ride from downtown Chetumal. **Combis** leave from Avenida Cristóbal Colón, behind the Museo de la Cultura Maya, roughly every half hour 6am-9pm daily (US$0.50, 15 minutes). If you've got a **car,** head east out of Chetumal on Boulevard Bahía, which becomes the main drag in Calderitas. Alternatively (though less scenic), take Avenida Insurgentes east until you get to the turnoff, and follow the signs from there.

OXTANKAH ARCHAEOLOGICAL ZONE

Oxtankah (8am-5pm daily, US$4) is a small archaeological site whose name means Between Branches, so called by early archaeologists after the many trees growing amid, and on top of, the structures. Relatively little is known about Oxtankah—including its true name—but it probably arose during the Classic era, between AD 300 and 600, and was dedicated primarily to trade and salt production. At its height, the city extended to the shores of Chetumal Bay and included the island of Tamalcab.

Oxtankah's principal structures were constructed in this period, suggesting it was a fairly robust city, but it was apparently abandoned around AD 600, for unknown reasons. The city was reoccupied by Maya settlers almost a thousand years later, in the 14th or 15th century, during which time a number of structures were expanded or enhanced. It was still occupied, mostly by modest earthen homes, when the first Spanish explorers arrived.

Some researchers have suggested the infamous Spaniard castaway Gonzalo Guerrero lived here; Guerrero was shipwrecked in this area in 1511 and adopted Maya ways, even marrying a chieftain's daughter. Their children are considered the New World's first mestizos, or mixed-race people.

In 1531, conquistador Alonso de Avila attempted to found a colonial city on the site, but he was driven out after two years of bitter conflict with local residents. He did manage to have a Franciscan chapel built, the skeleton of which remains, including an impressive eight-meter-tall (26-foot) arch.

Today, most of the excavated structures in Oxtankah surround two plazas: **Abejas** (Bees) plaza, the city's main ceremonial and elite residential center, and the somewhat smaller **Columnas** (Columns) plaza, whose large palace probably served an administrative function. Architecturally, the structures are more closely related to those of the Petén region (present-day Guatemala) than to Yucatecan ones, suggesting a close relationship with that area. There's a small **museum** on-site; signage is in Spanish only.

Getting There

Oxtankah is located seven kilometers (4 miles) north of Calderitas, about one kilometer (0.6 mile) off the bayside road. There's no public transportation to the site; a **cab** from Calderitas costs US$3 each way; one from Chetumal will run about US$18 round-trip, including wait time.

KOHUNLICH ARCHAEOLOGICAL ZONE

Swallowed by the jungle over the centuries, **Kohunlich** (8am-5pm daily, US$4) was first discovered in 1912 by American explorer Raymond Merwin, but it was not until the 1960s that excavation of the site began in earnest. Today, the ruins are in harmony with the surrounding vegetation; wandering through it, you'll be rewarded with more than 200 structures, stelae, and uncovered mounds that have trees growing out of them and moss spreading over their stones—a beautiful sight. Most date to the Late Preclassic (AD 100-200) through the Classic (AD 600-900) periods.

Kohunlich's most famous and compelling structure is the **Temple of the Masks.** Constructed in AD 500, it features six two-meter-tall (6.6-foot) stucco masks, believed to be representations of the Maya sun god, with star-incised eyes, mustaches, and nose plugs. Intriguingly, each is slightly different, leading some to speculate that they also represent successive members of the ruling dynasty; it would not have been unusual for the city's elite to draw an overt connection between themselves and a high god.

Southwest of the Temple of the Masks is **27 Escalones,** the largest and most impressive residential area in Kohunlich. Built on a cliff with a spectacular bird's-eye view of the jungle, it is one of the largest palaces in the Maya world, reached by climbing its namesake 27 steps. As you walk through the site, keep an eye out for *aguadas* (cisterns) that once were part of a complex system of Kohunlich's reservoirs.

Getting There

Kohunlich is located about 60 kilometers (37 miles) west of Chetumal. By **car,** take Highway 186 west and turn south (left) at the sign to Kohunlich. An 8.5-kilometer (5.3-mile) paved road leads straight to the site. There is no public transportation to the site.

DZIBANCHÉ AND KINICHNÁ ARCHAEOLOGICAL ZONES

If the crowds at Chichén Itzá and Tulum get you down, these picturesque twin ruins may

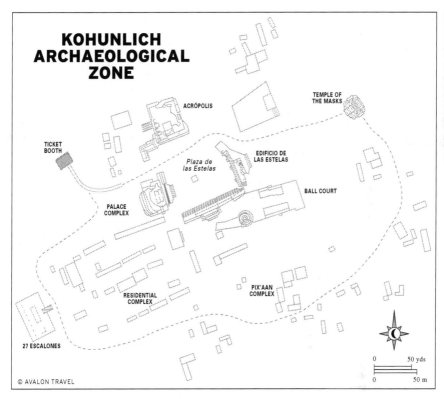

KOHUNLICH ARCHAEOLOGICAL ZONE

ACRÓPOLIS

TEMPLE OF THE MASKS

TICKET BOOTH

Plaza de las Estelas

EDIFICIO DE LAS ESTELAS

BALL COURT

PALACE COMPLEX

RESIDENTIAL COMPLEX

PIX'AAN COMPLEX

27 ESCALONES

0   50 yds

0   50 m

© AVALON TRAVEL

be the antidote you need. Dzibanché and its smaller neighbor, Kinichná, see very few visitors—it's not uncommon to have them to yourself, in fact—and feature modest-size temples in varying states of restoration. (A great many structures aren't excavated at all, but even they—abrupt tree-covered mounds—hold a certain mystery and appeal.)

Dzibanché

The larger of the two sites, Dzibanché is Yucatec Maya for Etched in Wood, a name created by archaeologists in reference to a wood lintel inscribed with hieroglyphics that was found in one of the primary temples. A date on the lintel reads AD 618, and the site seems to have flourished between AD 300 and AD 800. Archaeologists believe this area was occupied by a sprawling, widely dispersed city that covered some 40 square kilometers (25 square miles).

The site has three main plazas, each higher than the next. Dzibanché's namesake lintel is still in the temple atop **Structure VI,** also called the Building of the Lintels, facing one of the plazas. Unfortunately, climbing Structure VI is no longer allowed, but it's just one of several large pyramids here, the rest of which you can clamber up. The largest is **Structure II,** with an ornate temple at its summit where archaeologists found a tomb of a high-ranking leader (judging from the rich offering found with his remains). The steep stairways and lofty upper temples here are reminiscent of Tikal and other temples in the Petén area of present-day Guatemala, suggesting a strong connection between the two regions.

Kinichná

Kinichná (House of the Sun) has just one structure, but it's a biggie: a massive pyramid whose summit affords a great view of the surrounding countryside. The structure has three distinct levels, each built in a different era over the course of around 400 years. As you climb up, it's fascinating to observe how the craftsmanship and artistry changed—generally for the better—over the centuries. At the top is a stucco image of the sun god, hence the site's name. As in Structure II in Dzibanché, archaeologists uncovered a tomb here, this one containing the remains of two people and a cache of fine jade jewelry and figurines.

Practicalities

Dzibanché and Kinichná are open 8am-5pm daily; admission is US$4 and valid for both archaeological zones. There is no public transportation to or from the area, and precious little local traffic, so a **car** (or tour van) is essential. To get here, look for the turnoff 50 kilometers (31 miles) west of Chetumal on Highway 186, before reaching the town of Francisco Villa; from there it's 15 kilometers (9 miles) north down a bumpy dirt road. You'll reach Kinichná first, then Dzibanché about 2 kilometers (1.2 miles) later.

INLAND ARCHAEOLOGICAL ZONES

If you can drag yourself away from the beaches at Cancún or Tulum, or the diving on Isla Cozumel, a short trip inland will bring you to three of the Yucatán Peninsula's most intriguing ancient ruins—Chichén Itzá, Ek' Balam, and Cobá. Each is quite different from the other, and together they form an excellent introduction to Maya archaeology and architecture. Venturing inland also will

Highlights

LOOK FOR ◖ TO FIND RECOMMENDED SIGHTS, ACTIVITIES, DINING, AND LODGING.

◖ **Chichén Itzá Archaeological Zone:** Voted one of the New Seven Wonders of the World, the Yucatán's most famous ruin is all about hyperbole: the iconic star-aligned pyramid, the gigantic Maya ball court, even the crush of bikini-clad day-trippers from Cancún—be sure to arrive early (page 74).

◖ **Iglesia y Ex-Convento San Bernardino de Siena:** Located in a quiet corner of Valladolid, this elegant church has a spacious esplanade and beautiful interior, a small museum, plus a natural cenote inside the convent walls (page 85).

◖ **Ek' Balam Archaeological Zone:** A stunning stucco frieze with angel-like figures and a huge "monster mouth" is the highlight of this small, serene site near Valladolid. A nearby cenote makes for a cool après-ruins swim (page 93).

◖ **Cobá Archaeological Zone:** Just an hour from Tulum are the terrific jungle-cloaked ruins of Cobá, where you can climb the Yucatán's second-highest pyramid and rent bikes to get from temple to temple. Arrive early to enjoy the rich birdlife, then hit the nearby cenotes or monkey reserve for a great all-day outing (page 97).

◖ **Cenotes near Cobá:** A visit to Cobá just got better, with the opening of three impressive cenotes a short distance from the ruins. Each is unique, but all are massive caverns, with stalactites above and easy-to-use stairs descending to the cool shimmering water below (page 103).

give you an opportunity to sneak a peek at how ordinary Yucatecans, including modern-day Maya, live today.

Chichén Itzá (200 kilometers/124 miles from Cancún) is one of the most famous ruins in the Maya world, with a massive four-sided pyramid and the largest Maya ball court ever built. Just two hours from Cancún, it's inundated with tour groups; get there early to beat the crowds.

Even closer to the coast, but far less visited, is the small ruin of Ek' Balam (175 kilometers/109 miles from Cancún), boasting a beautiful stucco frieze partway up a massive pyramid. The frieze features winged priests and a gaping monster mouth that are so well preserved they look like they could be modern-day plaster art. A kilometer (0.6 mile) away, a cenote provides a welcome respite from the heat.

Less than an hour from Tulum—and a great alternative to the overcrowded ruins there—is the ancient city of Cobá (42 kilometers/26 miles from Tulum), home of the second-tallest known Maya pyramid. Unlike many other ruins, Cobá is ensconced in a thick tropical

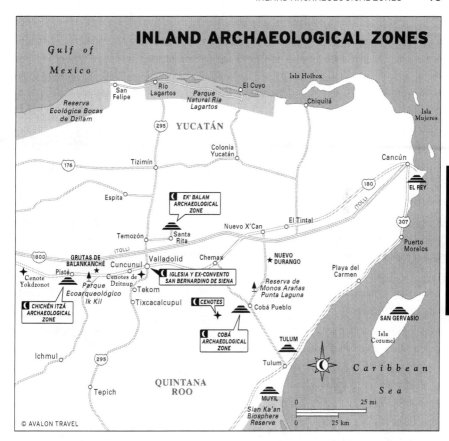

forest that teems with birdlife, including parrots and toucans.

PLANNING YOUR TIME

Chichén Itzá, Ek' Balam, and Cobá can each be reached as a day trip from Cancún or Tulum. You can visit all three in two or three days, staying overnight at hotels near the sites, or in Valladolid, an attractive and centrally located colonial town.

All the sites can be reached by bus or taxi,

especially Chichén Itzá and Cobá. But if you plan on visiting more than one site, a rental car may make your trip easier and more rewarding. You won't be tied to a bus schedule, and you'll be able to beat the crowds by getting to the sites bright and early. There also are numerous organized tours to Chichén Itzá from Cancún (though fewer to Cobá and Ek' Balam). While certainly convenient, many travelers find the large groups off-putting.

Chichén Itzá

Chichén Itzá is one of the finest archaeological sites in the northern part of the peninsula, and in all of Mesoamerica. It is also one of the most visited. Located just two hours from both Cancún and Mérida, the site is inundated by tour groups, many of them bikini-clad day-trippers on loan from the pool at their all-inclusive. That fact should not dissuade independent travelers from visiting—crowded or not, Chichén Itzá is a truly magnificent ruin and a must-see on any archaeology tour of the Yucatán. That said, you can make the most of your visit by arriving right when the gates open, so you can see the big stuff first and be exploring the outer areas by the time the tour buses start to roll in.

Pisté is a one-road town that is strangely underdeveloped considering it is just two kilometers (1.2 miles) from such an important and heavily visited site. The hotels and restaurants here are unremarkable, and there's not much to do or see in town.

◖ CHICHÉN ITZÁ ARCHAEOLOGICAL ZONE

Chichén Itzá (8am-5pm daily, US$14.75 including sound and light show) is a monumental archaeological site, remarkable for both its size and scope. The ruins include impressive palaces, temples, and altars, as well as the largest-known ball court in the Maya world. One of the most widely recognized (and heavily visited) ruins in the world, it was declared a World Heritage Site by UNESCO in 1988 and one of the New Seven Wonders of the World in 2007. In 2012, INAH (Instituto Nacional de Antropología e Historia) partnered with Google to photograph—by bicycle—the site for Google Street View maps.

History

What we call Chichén Itzá surely had another name when it was founded. The name means Mouth of the Well of the Itzá, but the Itzá, an illiterate and semi-nomadic group of uncertain origin, didn't arrive here until the 12th century. Before the Itzá, the area was controlled—or at least greatly influenced—by Toltec migrants who arrived from central Mexico around AD 1000. Most of Chichén's most notable structures, including its famous four-sided pyramid, and images like the reclining *chac-mool,* bear a striking resemblance to structures and images found at Tula, the ancient Toltec capital, in the state of Hidalgo. Before the Toltecs, the area was populated by Maya, evidenced by the Puuc- and Chenes-style design of the earliest structures here, such as the Nunnery and Casa Colorada.

The three major influences—Maya, Toltec, and Itzá—are indisputable, but the exact chronology and circumstances of those groups' interaction (or lack thereof) is one of the most hotly contested issues in Maya archaeology. Part of the difficulty in understanding Chichén Itzá more fully is that its occupants created very few stelae and left few Long Count dates on their monuments. In this way Chichén Itzá is different from virtually every other ancient city in the Yucatán. It's ironic, actually, that Chichén Itzá is the most widely recognized "Maya" ruin considering it was so deeply influenced by non-Maya cultures, and its history and architecture are so atypical of the region.

Chichén Itzá's influence ebbed and flowed over its many centuries of existence and occupation. It first peaked in the mid-9th century, or Late Classic period, when it eclipsed Cobá as the dominant power in the northern Yucatán region. The effects of a widespread collapse of Maya cities to the south (like Calakmul, Tikal, and Palenque) reached Chichén Itzá in the late 900s, and it too collapsed abruptly. The city rose again under Toltec and later Itzá influence, but went into its final decline after an internal dispute led to the rise of Mayapán, which would come to control much of the Yucatán Peninsula. Chichén Itzá was all but abandoned

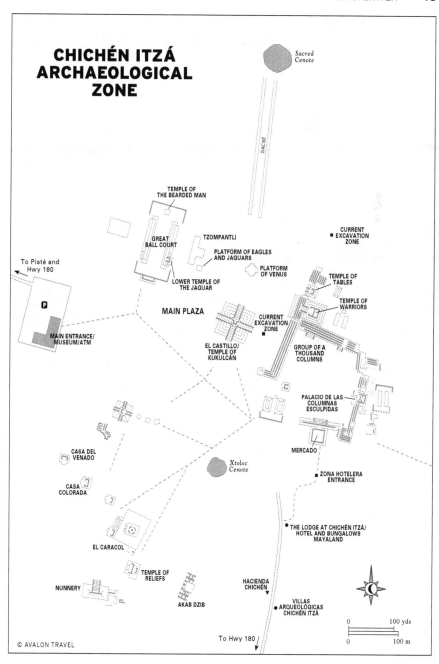

CHICHÉN ITZÁ ARCHAEOLOGICAL ZONE

Sacred Cenote

SACBÉ

TEMPLE OF THE BEARDED MAN

CURRENT EXCAVATION ZONE

GREAT BALL COURT

TZOMPANTLI

PLATFORM OF EAGLES AND JAGUARS

PLATFORM OF VENUS

TEMPLE OF TABLES

To Pisté and Hwy 180

LOWER TEMPLE OF THE JAGUAR

TEMPLE OF WARRIORS

MAIN PLAZA

CURRENT EXCAVATION ZONE

P

MAIN ENTRANCE/ MUSEUM/ATM

EL CASTILLO/ TEMPLE OF KUKULCÁN

GROUP OF A THOUSAND COLUMNS

PALACIO DE LAS COLUMNAS ESCULPIDAS

CASA DEL VENADO

MERCADO

Xtoloc Cenote

ZONA HOTELERA ENTRANCE

CASA COLORADA

THE LODGE AT CHICHÉN ITZÁ/ HOTEL AND BUNGALOWS MAYALAND

EL CARACOL

TEMPLE OF RELIEFS

HACIENDA CHICHÉN

NUNNERY

AKAB DZIB

VILLAS ARQUEOLÓGICAS CHICHÉN ITZÁ

To Hwy 180

0   100 yds

0   100 m

© AVALON TRAVEL

The Maya Collapse

Something went terribly wrong for the Maya between the years AD 800 and 900. Hundreds of Classic Maya cities were abandoned, monarchies disappeared, and the population fell by millions, mainly due to death and plummeting birthrates. The collapse was widespread, but was most dramatic in the Southern Lowlands, a swath of tropical forest stretching from the Gulf of Mexico to Honduras and including once-glorious cities such as Palenque, Tikal, and Copán. (Archaeologists first suspected a collapse after noticing a sudden drop-off in inscriptions; it has been confirmed through excavations of peasant dwellings from before and after that period.)

There are many theories for the collapse, varying from climate change and epidemic diseases to foreign invasion and peasant revolt. In his carefully argued book *The Fall of the Ancient Maya* (Thames and Hudson, 2002), archaeologist and professor of anthropology at Pennsylvania State University David Webster suggests it was a series of conditions, rather than a single event, that led to the collapse.

To a certain degree, it was the very success of Maya cities during the Classic era that set the stage for their demise. Webster points to a population boom just before the collapse, which would have left agricultural lands dangerously depleted just as demand spiked. Classic-era farming techniques were ill-suited to meet the challenge; in particular, the lack of draft animals kept productivity low, meaning Maya farmers could not generate large surpluses of corn and other food. (Even if they could, storage was difficult given the hot, humid climate.) The lack of animals also limited how far away farmers could cultivate land and still be able to transport their crops to the city center; as a result, available land was overused. As Webster puts it, "too many farmers [growing] too many crops on too much of the landscape left the Classic Maya world acutely vulnerable to an environmental catastrophe, such as drought or crop disease."

Certain kingdoms reached their tipping point before others (prompting some to launch 11th-hour military campaigns against weakened rivals), but few escaped the wave of malnutrition, disease, lower birthrates, and outright starvation that seems to have swept across the Maya world in the 9th century. Kings and nobility would have faced increasing unrest and insurrection—after all, their legitimacy was based on their ability to induce the gods to bestow rain, fertility, and prosperity—further destabilizing the social structure and food supply.

The collapse was not universal, of course, and the fall of lowland powers gave other city-states an opportunity to expand and gain influence. But the Maya world was dramatically and permanently changed by it; the grand cities built by the Classic Maya were abandoned to the jungle, most never to be reoccupied, and, as Webster notes, "Cortés and his little army almost starved in 1525 while crossing a wilderness that had supported millions of people seven centuries earlier."

by the early 1200s, though it remained an important religious pilgrimage site even after the arrival of the Spanish.

El Castillo/Temple of Kukulcán

The most dramatic structure in Chichén Itzá is El Castillo (The Castle), also known as the Temple of Kukulcán. At 24 meters (79 feet), it's the tallest structure on the site, and certainly the most recognizable. Dating to around AD 850, El Castillo was built according to strict astronomical guidelines. There are nine levels,

which, divided by the central staircase, make for 18 platforms, the number of months in the Maya calendar. Each of the four sides has 91 steps, which, added together along with the platform on top, total 365—one for each day of the year. And there are 52 inset panels on each face of the structure, equal to the number of years in each cycle of the Calendar Round.

On the spring and autumn equinoxes (March 21 and September 22), the afternoon sun lights up a bright zigzag strip on the outside wall of the north staircase as well as the giant

El Castillo, Chichén Itzá's famous main pyramid, as seen from the nearby Group of a Thousand Columns

serpent heads at the base, giving the appearance of a serpent slithering down the steps. Chichén Itzá is mobbed during those periods, especially by spiritual-minded folks seeking communion with the ancient Maya. The effect also occurs in the days just before and after the equinox, and there are significantly fewer people blocking the view.

Climbing El Castillo used to be a given for any visit to Chichén Itzá, and the views from its top level are breathtaking. However, an elderly tourist died in 2005 after tumbling from near the top of the pyramid to the ground. The accident, combined with longtime warnings from archaeologists that the structure was being irreparably eroded by the hundreds of thousands of visitors who climbed it yearly, prompted officials to close it off. Pyramids at other sites have been restricted as well, and it's looking more and more like a standard policy at Maya archaeological zones.

Deep inside El Castillo and accessed by way of a steep, narrow staircase are several chambers; inside one is a red-painted, jade-studded bench in the figure of a jaguar, which may have served as a throne of sorts. You used to be able to climb the stairs to see the chambers and throne—a fascinating, albeit humid and highly claustrophobic affair—but access was closed at the same time climbing the pyramid was prohibited.

Great Ball Court

Chichén Itzá's famous Great Ball Court is the largest ball court in Mesoamerica by a wide margin. The playing field is 135 meters (443 feet) by 65 meters (213 feet), with two parallel walls 8 meters high (26 feet) and scoring rings in impossibly high perches in the center. The players would've had to hit a 12-pound rubber ball through the rings using only their elbows, wrists, and hips (they wore heavy padding). The game likely lasted for hours; at the game's end, the captain of one team—or even the whole team—was apparently sacrificed, possibly by decapitation. There's disagreement about *which* team got the axe, however. Some say it was the losers—otherwise the game's best players would constantly be wiped out. Some argue that it was the winners, and that being sacrificed would have been the ultimate honor. Of course, it's likely the game varied from city to city and evolved over the many centuries it was played. Along the walls, reliefs depict the ball game and sacrifices.

On the outside of the ball court, the **Lower Temple of the Jaguar** has incredibly fine relief carvings depicting the Maya creation myth. An upper temple is off-limits to visitors, but is decorated with a variety of carvings and remnants of what were likely colorful murals.

The Platforms

As you make your way from the ball court to the Temple of Warriors, you'll pass the gruesome **Tzompantli** (Wall of Skulls). A low T-shaped platform, it is decorated on all sides with row upon row of carved skulls, most with eyes staring out of the large sockets. Among the skulls are images of warriors holding the heads of decapitated victims, skeletons intertwined with snakes, and eagles eating human hearts (a common image in Toltec design, further evidence of their presence here). It is presumed that ceremonies performed on this platform culminated in a sacrificial death for the victim, the head then left on display, perhaps with others already in place. It's estimated that the platform was built AD 1050-1200. Nearby, the **Platform of Venus** and **Platform of Eagles and Jaguars** are smaller square structures, each with low stairways on all four sides, which were likely used for ritualistic music and dancing.

Sacred Cenote

This natural well is 300 meters (984 feet) north of the main structures, along the remains of a *sacbé* (raised stone road) constructed during the Classic period. Almost 60 meters (197 feet) in diameter and 30 meters (98.4 feet) down to the surface of the water, it was a place for sacrifices, mostly to Chaac, the god of rain, who was believed to live in its depths. The cenote has been dredged

and scoured by divers numerous times, beginning as early as 1900, and the remains of scores of victims, mostly children and young adults, have been recovered, as well as innumerable jade and stone artifacts. (Most are now displayed at the Museo Nacional de Antropología in Mexico City.) On the edge of the cenote is a ruined sweat bath, probably used for purification rituals before sacrificial ceremonies. The name Chichén Itzá (Mouth of the Well of the Itzá) is surely derived from this deeply sacred cenote, and it remained an important Maya pilgrimage site well into the Spanish conquest.

Temple of Warriors and Group of a Thousand Columns

The Temple of Warriors is where some of the distinctive reclining *chac-mool* figures are found. However, its name comes from the rectangular monoliths in front, which are carved on all sides with images of warriors. (Some are also prisoners, their hands tied behind their backs.) This temple is also closed to entry, and it can be hard to appreciate the fading images from the rope perimeter. You may be able to get a closer look from the temple's south side, where you can easily make out the figures' expressions and dress (though access is sometimes blocked there as well). The south side is impressive for its facade, too, where a series of well-preserved human and animal figures adorn the lower portion, while above, human faces emerge from serpents' mouths, framed by eagle profiles, with masks of Chaac, the hook-nosed god of rain, on the corners.

The aptly named Group of a Thousand Columns is adjacent to the Temple of Warriors. It's perfectly aligned cylindrical columns likely held up a grand roof structure.

Across the plaza, the **Palacio de las Columnas Esculpidas** (Palace of Sculptured Columns) also has cylindrical columns, but with intricate carvings, suggesting this was the ceremonial center of this portion of the complex. Continuing through the trees, you'll reach the **Mercado** (market). The name is purely speculative, though it's easy to imagine a breezy bustling market here, protected from the sun under a wood and *palapa* roof built atop the structure's remarkably high columns.

Osario, El Caracol, and the Nunnery

From the market, bear left (away from El Castillo, just visible through the trees) until you meet the path leading to the site's southern entrance. You'll pass the **Osario** (ossuary), also known as the Tomb of the High Priest. Like a miniature version of El Castillo, the pyramid at one time had four stairways on each side and a temple at the crest. From the top platform, a vertical passageway leads into a chamber where seven tombs were discovered, along with numerous copper and jade artifacts indicating the deceased were of special importance (and hence the temple's name). Continuing on, you'll pass two more large structures, **Casa del Venado** (House of the Deer) and **Casa Colorada** (Red House).

The highlight of this portion of Chichén Itzá is **El Caracol** (The Snail Shell), also known as the Observatory, and perhaps the most graceful structure at Chichén Itzá. A two-tiered circular structure is set atop a broad rectangular platform, with window slits facing south and west, and another aligned according to the path of the moon during the spring equinoxes. Ancient astronomers used structures like this one to track celestial events and patterns—the orbits of the Moon and Venus, and the coming of solar and lunar eclipses, for example—with uncanny accuracy.

Beyond El Caracol is the **Nunnery,** so-named by Spanish explorers who thought it looked like convents back home. Judging from its size, location, and many rooms, the Nunnery was probably an administrative palace. Its exuberant facades show strong Chenes influence, another example of the blending of styles in Chichén Itzá.

Sound and Light Show

Though it was closed for retooling at the time of research, the site puts on a nightly high-tech sound and light show at 7pm in the winter (Oct.-Apr.) and at 8pm in the summer (May-Sept.). The fee to enter is included in the general admission; if you'd like to see the show the night before you visit the ruins, buy a US$10 partial entrance—*not* the show-only ticket—and keep your stub for credit the next morning. (Just tell the ticket seller your plan, and you'll get the right ticket. If you're only interested in the show and want to skip the ruins, the price is US$6.) The sound and light show is presented in Spanish, but for an additional US$3.25 you can rent headphones with translations in English, French, German, and Italian.

Practicalities

The grounds are open 8am-5pm daily. Admission is US$14.75 per person, plus US$3.75 to enter with a video camera; parking is US$1.80. The fee includes entrance to the ruins and the sound and light show, but there is no discount if you don't go to the latter.

Guides can be hired at the entrance according to fixed and clearly marked prices: US$42 for a two-hour tour in Spanish, US$50 in English, French, Italian, or German. Prices are per group, which can include up to eight people. Tips are customary and not included in the price. The visitors center has restrooms, an ATM, free luggage storage, a café, a bookstore, a gift shop, and an information center.

GRUTAS DE BALANKANCHÉ

Six kilometers (3.7 miles) east of Chichén Itzá, the **Balankanché Caves** (9am-5pm daily, US$8.50, child under 9 free) are a disappointment. The 1959 excavation of the caves by *National Geographic* archaeologist Dr. E. Wyllys Andrews uncovered numerous artifacts and ceremonial sites, giving researchers a better understanding of ancient Maya cosmology, especially related to the notion of *Xibalba* (the underworld). Nowadays, the caves are basically a tourist trap—a wide path meandering 500 meters (0.3 mile) down a tunnel with urns and other artifacts supposedly set up in their original locations. Wires and electric lights illuminate the path, but the recorded narration does nothing of the sort—it's so garbled you can hardly understand it, no matter what language it's in.

Entry times are fixed according to language: Spanish hourly 9am-4pm; English at 11am, 1pm, and 3pm; and French at 10am. A minimum of six visitors are needed for the tour to depart.

PARQUE ECOARQUEOLÓGICO IK KIL

Three kilometers (1.9 miles) east of Pisté, the centerpiece of the **Ik Kil Eco-Archaeological Park** (Carr. Mérida-Cancún Km. 122, tel. 985/851-0002, cenote_ikkil@hotmail.com, 8am-6pm daily Apr.-Oct., 8am-5pm daily Nov.-Mar., US$6 adult, US$3 child) is the immense, perfectly round **Cenote Sagrado Azul,** with a partial stone roof. Although the cenote is real, the alterations to its natural state—supported walls, a set of stairs leading you in, a waterfall—make it feel pretty artificial. While not representative of the typical cenote experience, this is a good option if you are traveling with small children and need a spot to cool off. Lockers are available for US$2.50. The cenote and on-site restaurant (breakfast US$6.25, lunch buffet US$12.50) get packed with tour groups 12:30pm-2:30pm; try visiting outside those times for a mellower experience. Better yet, stay at one of the on-site bungalows (US$104 s/d with a/c).

ACCOMMODATIONS

A handful of upscale hotels make up the small Zona Hotelera on the east side of Chichén Itzá, complete with its own entrance to the ruins. Nearby, in the town of Pisté, there are also a few budget and mid-range options. Be sure to reserve early during the spring and fall equinoxes. All the options below (except Ik Kil) have Wi-Fi available, though often in the reception area only. Book rooms online for the lowest rates.

US$25-50

On the eastern end of Pisté toward the ruins, **Pirámide Inn** (Calle 15 No. 30, tel. 985/851-0115, www.chichen.com, US$42 s/d) is a low,

sprawling hotel with large rooms that are clean though a bit dark. The decor is distinctly 1970s den, with some rooms sporting bubblegum paint jobs and lacquered brick walls. The air conditioners appear to be from the same era, and can be loud. Cement seating frames a pool in a pleasant fruit tree garden. Backpackers can **camp** or **rent a hammock** here (US$4-8 pp) with access to the pool and cleanish shared bathrooms.

Posada Olalde (Calle 6 at Calle 17, tel. 985/851-0086, US$21/29 s/d with fan) is the best budget option in town. Seven simple rooms are brightly painted, with a long shared porch facing a leafy courtyard. The hotel also has four pressed-earth bungalows, which sound nice but have saggy beds, bad light, and a dank feel—better to stick with the rooms. The dirt access road is easy to miss—look for it just west of (and on the opposite side of the street from) the OXXO mini-mart. There's street parking only.

Posada Chac-Mool (Calle 15 s/n, tel. 985/851-0270, US$25 d with fan, US$33 with a/c) has basic hot-water rooms with thin towels, loose-fill pillows, and beds in various age brackets. Still, it does have Wi-Fi and parking, and management will bargain if it's slow.

US$50-100

Affiliated with Best Western, **Hotel Chichén** (Calle 15 s/n, tel. 985/851-0022, US$71-112 s/d with a/c) is the nicest hotel in downtown Pisté, featuring king or two queen bed rooms with comfortable furnishings, large modern bathrooms, and simple Mexican decor. The less-expensive rooms face the street and can be noisy, while the top-floor ones are larger and overlook the hotel's attractive garden and pool area. There's a guest computer, plus a cavernous restaurant (7am-11pm daily) that's often packed with tour groups.

The **Hotel Dolores Alba Chichén** (Carr. Mérida-Cancún Km. 122, tel. 985/858-1555, www.doloresalba.com, US$54-58 s/d with a/c) is one of the best deals in the area, especially given its choice location three kilometers (1.9 miles) east of the ruins, one

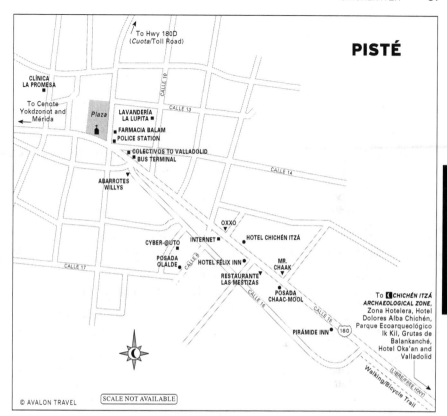

To Hwy 180D
(*Cuota*/Toll Road)

PISTÉ

CLÍNICA
LA PROMESA

To Cenote
Yokdzonot and
← Mérida

Plaza

CALLE 10

CALLE 13

LAVANDERÍA
LA LUPITA ■

■ FARMACIA BALAM
POLICE STATION

■ COLECTIVOS TO VALLADOLID
● BUS TERMINAL

CALLE 14

ABARROTES
WILLYS

OXXO

CYBER-@UTO   INTERNET ■   ● HOTEL CHICHÉN ITZÁ

POSADA
OLALDE ●   HOTEL FÉLIX INN ●   MR.
CHAAK

CALLE 17

CALLE 8

RESTAURANTE
LAS MESTIZAS

● POSADA
CHAAC-MOOL

CALLE 16

CALLE 15

To **◖** CHICHÉN ITZÁ
ARCHAEOLOGICAL ZONE,
Zona Hotelera, Hotel
Dolores Alba Chichén,
Parque Ecoarqueológico
Ik Kil, Grutas de
Balankanché,
Hotel Oka'an and
Valladolid

PIRÁMIDE INN ●   180

Walking/Bicycle Trail

(LIBRE/FREE HWY)

© AVALON TRAVEL   SCALE NOT AVAILABLE

kilometer (0.6 mile) from the Balankanché Caves, and across the street from the Parque Ecoarqueológico Ik Kil. Rooms are spotless and smallish, with good beds and simple tile work on the walls to spiff up the decor, and tour groups are situated in an area separate from independent travelers. The hotel has a pleasant outdoor restaurant (7am-10pm daily, US$5-10) and two large swimming pools—the one in back has a mostly natural stone bottom, with holes and channels reminiscent of an ocean reef, which is perfect for kids with active imaginations. Other amenities include continental breakfast and a computer for rent in reception. The hotel also provides free shuttle service to the ruins during the day (though not back); it's US$1.70

per person round-trip for an evening shuttle to the sound and light show.

The **Hotel Fenix Inn** (Calle 15 btwn Calles 2 and 4, tel. 985/851-0033, US$54-63 s/d with a/c) features six rooms that open onto a lush garden with an aboveground pool and a *palapa*-roofed restaurant. Though overpriced, the rooms have nice wood furnishings from Michoacán, newish TVs, and silent air-conditioning. Still, reception seems to be permanently MIA, and it's a bit dark and dreary here in the evenings.

US$100-150
Set in a lush forest, **◖ Parque Ecoarqueológico Ik Kil** (Carr. Mérida-Cancún Km. 122, tel. 985/858-1525, US$104 s/d with a/c) offers 14

modern and ultra-comfortable bungalows. All are spacious and have whirlpool tubs and comfortable beds, and a handful sport pull-out sofas. Silent air-conditioning and a private porch make it all the better. Guests get unlimited use of the on-site cenote, including after hours. It's a fantastic value, especially for those traveling with kids.

Villas Arqueológicas Chichén Itzá (Zona Hotelera, Carr. Mérida-Valladolid Km. 120, tel. 985/851-0187, toll-free Mex. tel. 800/557-7755, www.villasarqueologicas.com.mx, US$104 s/d with a/c, US$154 suite with a/c) is a pleasant two-story hotel with a mellow ambience. Boxy but nice rooms are set around a lush courtyard with an inviting L-shaped pool. A library/TV room with comfy couches and a variety of reading material—from romance novels to archaeology books—also faces the courtyard. A decent restaurant and a tennis court (with nighttime lighting and racquets to borrow) are on-site too. Very tall folks should note that alcove walls bracket the ends of the beds.

A new holistic retreat center with two dozen rooms in a forest setting, **Hotel Oka'an** (Carr. Mérida-Cancún Km. 122, cell. tel. 985/105-8402, www.hotelokaan.com, US$115-200 s/d with a/c, US$240-280 suite with a/c) beckons with a full spa, yoga workshops, and the occasional spiritual ceremony. Ample standard rooms have balconies with hammocks, and corner units have an extra set of picture windows letting in more light. Larger and more luxurious bungalows have decorative stone butterflies and turtles detailing the floors and earthy contemporary architecture, plus private terraces. Continental breakfast is served in a draped open-air restaurant (8am-10pm daily, US$7.50-10), offering regional, international, and vegetarian options. For post-ruin lounging, an infinity pool cascades into smaller shaded basins, but don't miss the killer view from the *mirador* terrace—Chichén Itzá's El Castillo pops up over the (arduously manicured) treeline. Look for the road marquis just west of the Hotel Dolores Alba and continue 1.5 kilometers (0.9 mile) on an unpaved road; it's a US$8 taxi ride from Pisté.

Over US$150

Once the headquarters for the Carnegie Institute's Chichén Itzá expedition, the **Hacienda Chichén Resort** (Zona Hotelera, Carr. Mérida-Valladolid Km. 120, tel. 999/920-8407, toll-free U.S. tel. 877/631-4005, www.haciendachichen.com, US$169-265 with a/c) is now a tranquil hotel set in a lush tropical garden. Newer units are quite comfortable, with tile floors, exposed beam ceilings, and wood furnishings. Many of the older units occupy the original cottages used by archaeologists who conducted their first excavations of Chichén Itzá—very cool in theory, though the cinder-block walls and pervasive mustiness diminish the charm. Still, the latter are usually booked solid. Be sure to wander the grounds with an eye for the original hacienda (blocks from the ruins are incorporated into the main building) and narrow-gauge railroad tracks that were used to transport artifacts from Chichén Itzá. A pool, full-service spa (7:30am-9:30pm daily), and a fine dining room are also nice.

The Lodge at Chichén Itzá (Zona Hotelera, Carr. Mérida-Valladolid Km. 120, tel. 998/887-9162, toll-free Mex. tel. 800/719-5495, toll-free U.S. tel. 800/235-4079, www.mayaland.com, US$175-433 s/d with a/c) is part of the larger Mayaland resort, which is literally at the rear entrance to the ruins; guests and nonguests must pass through the resort (and two of its gift shops) to get to the ticket booth. The grounds are gorgeous: 100 acres of tamed tropical jungle featuring walking and horseback riding trails, a full-service spa, three restaurants, and three pools. The lodges *palapa*-roofed bungalows are pleasant (if somewhat dated), with stained-glass windows, hardwood furniture, and terraces with rocking chairs. Lodge accommodations are typically reserved for independent travelers, and their location—including a separate access road and parking lot—is fairly removed from Mayaland proper, where groups are handled. Still, you're bound to encounter various loud flocks of day-trippers during your stay, especially in the reception area or restaurant, which diminishes the charm for some.

FOOD

Eating options are pretty limited in Pisté but improve somewhat if you have a car and can get to and from the large hotels.

⟨ Restaurante Las Mestizas (Calle 15 s/n, tel. 985/851-0069, 7:30am-10:30pm daily, US$4-12) is the best place to eat in Pisté, with an airy, colonial-style interior and tasty, good-sized portions. The food is classic Yucatecan fare, from *panuchos* to *pollo pibil*. Service is exceptional.

Excellent for a hearty breakfast before exploring the ruins, the shady garden deck at **⟨ Mr. Chaak** (Calle 15 s/n, tel. 985/851-0081, 7am-10pm daily, US$6-7) hits the spot with a nice choice of *chilaquiles,* eggs, and French toast or waffles, served up with strong espresso drinks and frappés. Focaccia sandwiches and light Yucatecan fare round out the menu, which uses fresh herbs grown on-site and patisserie bread delivered from Mérida. Free Wi-Fi is available.

Set in a 16th-century hacienda, the **⟨ Hacienda Chichén Resort's restaurant** (Zona Hotelera, tel. 999/920-8407, 7am-10pm daily, US$14-25) is a soothing place to eat after a long day at the ruins. The menu is varied—Yucatecan specialties, pastas, sandwiches—and on the occasional evening, a trio plays regional music. Some of the produce is grown in its beautiful organic garden.

If you can stand the tour groups, the lunch buffet at **Hotel and Bungalows Mayaland** (Zona Hotelera, Carr. Mérida-Valladolid Km. 120, tel. 985/851-0100, noon-4:30pm daily, US$13) offers a variety of hot and cold dishes that will definitely fill you up. Live music, ballet *folklórico* shows, and outdoor seating are nice touches.

For groceries, **Abarrotes Willy's** (Calle 2 s/n, 7am-10pm daily) has the best selection and prices in town. Follow the pulsating music a block southeast of the plaza.

INFORMATION AND SERVICES

There is no tourist office in Pisté; hotel receptionists are sometimes helpful—depends who you get—as are other travelers. Pisté also doesn't have a bank, but there are three local ATMs: inside the OXXO market, across the street from OXXO, and in Chichén Itzá's visitors complex.

Emergency Services

The **police** have an office (tel. 985/851-0365) in the Palacio Municipal, facing the church. An officer is on duty 24 hours a day, and there's usually one waving through traffic near the plaza. **Clínica La Promesa** (Calle 14 btwn Calles 13 and 15, tel. 985/851-0005, 24 hours) is one of two clinics in town. For anything serious, you're better off going to Mérida or Cancún. **Farmacia Balam** (Calle 15 s/n, 985/851-0358, 7am-midnight daily) is just north of the Palacio Municipal.

Media and Communications

In the middle of town, across from the OXXO mini-mart, a **no-name Internet place** (Calle 15 s/n, 10am-10pm daily, US$0.80/hour) has a fast connection plus international telephone service (US$0.40/minute to U.S. and Canada, US$0.60/minute to Europe).

Off the road that parallels the main drag, and across from the cemetery, **Ciber-@uto** (Calle 4A, 9am-7pm daily, US$1/hour), is a combination Internet café-and-car-wash run out of a family home.

Laundry

Lavandería La Lupita (Calle 10 near Calle 13, 8am-8pm Mon.-Sat.) charges US$1.70 per kilo (2.2 pounds) to wash and dry clothes; they'll do same-day service if you drop your load off first thing in the morning.

GETTING THERE AND AROUND
Bus

Pisté's small **bus terminal** (8:30am-5:30pm daily, cash only) is just southeast of the Palacio Municipal, and about 2.5 kilometers (1.5 miles) from the entrance to Chichén Itzá. There is also a **ticket office** in the gift shop at the ruins (tel. 985/851-0377, 9am-5pm daily). (The visitors center at Chichén Itzá also has **free luggage storage,** which makes it easy to catch a bus right after visiting the ruins.) **All first-class departures leave from Chichén Itzá only.** Second-class departure times listed here are for the terminal in Pisté. Second-class buses coming and going between 8am and 5:30pm stop at both the terminal and the parking lot at the ruins. If planning to catch a second-class bus at the ruins, keep in mind that buses headed toward Cancún stop at the ruins slightly after the listed times, while those bound for Mérida pass by slightly earlier. Most bus service to and from Pisté and Chichén Itzá is on Oriente, ADO's second-class line, but the few first-class buses are worth the extra cost.

- Cancún: One daily first-class bus (US$16, 3.5 hours) at 4:30pm; second-class buses (US$10, 4-4.5 hours) every 30-60 minutes 5:30am-11:30pm.

- Cobá: For the town and archaeological site (US$5, 2.5 hours), take the second-class Tulum bus at 7:30am; the first-class buses do not stop there.

- Mérida: First-class buses (US$9.50, 2 hours) leave at 2:20pm and 5:15pm; second-class buses (US$5.50, 2.5 hours) every 30-60 minutes 6am-11:30pm.

- Playa del Carmen: Second-class buses (US$11, 4 hours) from Pisté at 1pm and 7pm Friday, 1pm Saturday, and 7pm Sunday.

- Tulum: First-class buses (US$12, 2.5 hours) leave at 8:25am and 4:30pm; one second-class departure at 7:30am (US$6.25, 3.5 hours).

- Valladolid: First-class buses (US$5, 50 minutes) at 11:20am and 4:30pm; second-class service (US$2, 1 hour) every 30-60 minutes 5:30am-11:30pm.

White *colectivos* (US$2, 40 minutes) leave for Valladolid every 30 minutes 7am-6pm from in front of the bus terminal.

Car

Chichén Itzá lies adjacent to Highway 180, 40 kilometers (25 miles) west of Valladolid, 120 kilometers (75 miles) east of Mérida, and 200 kilometers (124 miles) west of Cancún. For drivers, the quickest way to get there is via the *cuota,* a large modern freeway extending from Cancún most of the way to Mérida, with a well-marked exit for Chichén Itzá and Pisté. There's a price for speed and convenience, though: The toll from Mérida is just US$7, but a whopping US$33 from Cancún. You can also take the old *carretera libre* (free highway) all or part of the way; it's in reasonably good condition but takes much longer, mainly because you pass through numerous small villages and seemingly innumerable *topes* (speed bumps).

Air

Aeropuerto Internacional Chichén Itzá is 16 kilometers (9.9 miles) east of Pisté, between the towns of Xcalacot and Kaua. Inaugurated in April 2000, it is one of the most modern airports in the country, with an 1,800-meter (5,900-foot) runway capable of receiving 747 jets. Although it initially received dozens of regular and charter flights, its license was suspended in 2001. Today it stands virtually empty, receiving only a smattering of charters, mostly from Cancún, Cozumel, and Chetumal, though rumors of restarting service crop up from time to time.

Valladolid

Valladolid draws tourists because of its mellow colonial atmosphere and its central location: 30 minutes from the archaeological zones of Chichén Itzá and Ek' Balam, an hour from the ruins at Cobá and the flamingo reserve in Río Lagartos, and two hours from Mérida, Cancún, and Tulum. It's an easy bus or car ride to any of these destinations, restaurants and hotels are reasonably priced, and you have the advantage of staying in a colonial Mexican town. If you're en route to one of the regional sites or simply want to have a small-city experience, consider spending a night here—you're sure to be happily surprised.

HISTORY

The site of several Maya revolts against the Spanish, Valladolid was conquered in 1543 by Francisco de Montejo, cousin of the like-named Spaniard who founded Mérida. It was once the Maya city of Zací. Montejo brutalized its inhabitants and crushed their temples, building large churches and homes in their place. It is perhaps not surprising, then, that the Caste War started in Valladolid, and that the city played an important role in the beginning of the Mexican Revolution. Today, Valladolid is a charming colonial town with a rich history and strong Maya presence.

ORIENTATION

Valladolid is easy to get around. It's laid out in a grid pattern with even-numbered streets running north to south, odd-numbered streets running east to west. The central plaza at the center of the city is bordered by Calles 39, 40, 41, and 42.

SIGHTS

◀ Iglesia y Ex-Convento San Bernardino de Siena

Located at the end of the Calzada de los Frailes, the **Iglesia y Ex-Convento San Bernardino de Siena** (Calle 41-A, tel. 985/856-2160, 7am-1pm

and 5pm-8pm daily) is one of Valladolid's most attractive structures. Built by Franciscan missionaries between 1552 and 1560, the church is entered through a series of arches, and the facade, covered in a checkerboard-like stucco pattern, rises into a squat tower with turrets. Inside, there are original 16th-century frescoes, catacombs, and crypts. Annexed to it, the ex-monastery has rooms radiating from a center courtyard that features, uniquely, a cenote. Called Ziis-Há (Cold Water), the cenote helped the monks be self-reliant. In 2004, an INAH-funded exploration of the cenote resulted in the discovery of 164 rifles and one cannon. Although neither the age nor the origin of the arms has been disclosed, it is speculated that they date from the mid-1800s, when the monastery was used as a fortress during the Maya uprisings. Mass is held at 7am and 7pm Monday-Friday; 7am, 8:30am, and 7pm Saturday; and at 7am, 8am, 9am, 10am, 5pm, 6pm, 7pm, and 8:30pm on Sunday. Special permission is required to visit the monastery; call ahead or ask in the church office.

Casa de los Venados

If you have even a passing interest in Mexican folk art—or an infatuation with exquisite colonial buildings—make sure to schedule a post-breakfast visit to the **House of the Deer** (Calle 40 btwn Calles 41 and 43, 985/856-2289, www.casadelosvenados.com, 10am tour daily, US$5 donation requested). After an architectural award-winning, eight-year remodel of this early 17th-century house, the American couple who own it had so many visitors stopping by to see their extensive art collection that they now welcome visitors at 10am daily for tours of their mansion home and their incredible 3,000-piece collection—the largest Mexican folk art collection not owned by a museum. The pieces span John and Dorianne Venator's 50 years of seeking out and commissioning *catrinas,* clay sculptures, wood carvings, paintings, and other

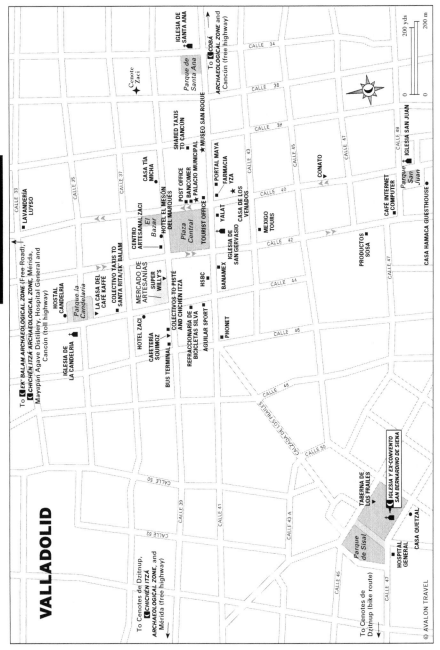

VALLADOLID

To Cenotes de Dzitnup, CHICHÉN ITZÁ ARCHAEOLOGICAL ZONE, and Mérida (free highway)

To Cenotes de Dzitnup (bike route)

To EK' BALAM ARCHAEOLOGICAL ZONE (Free Road), CHICHÉN ITZÁ ARCHAEOLOGICAL ZONE, Mérida, Mayapán Agave Distillery, Hospital General and Cancún (toll highway)

To COBÁ ARCHAEOLOGICAL ZONE and Cancún (free highway)

Cenote Zaci

Parque de Santa Ana

IGLESIA DE SANTA ANA

LAVANDERIA LUYSO

CALLE 33

CALLE 34

CALLE 35

CALLE 36

CALLE 37

CALLE 38

CALLE 39

CALLE 40

CALLE 41

CALLE 42

CALLE 43

CALLE 43 A

CALLE 44

CALLE 45

CALLE 46

CALLE 47

CALLE 48

CALLE 49

CALLE 50

CALLE 52

CALZADA DE LOS FRAILES

HOSTAL CANDELARIA

Parque la Candelaria

IGLESIA DE LA CANDELRIA

LA CASA DEL CAFÉ KAFFE

COLECTIVO TAXIS TO SANTA RITA/EK' BALAM

HOTEL ZACI

CAFETERÍA SQUIMOZ

BUS TERMINAL

CENTRO ARTESANAL ZACI

MERCADO DE ARTESANIAS

SUPER WILLY'S

COLECTIVOS TO PISTE AND CHICHEN ITZA

REFRACCIONARIA DE BICICLETAS SILVA

AGUILAR SPORT

PHONET

El Bazar

HSBC

BANAMEX

HOTEL EL MESÓN DEL MARQUÉS

POST OFFICE

BANCOMER

PALACIO MUNICIPAL

Plaza Central

TOURIST OFFICE

YALAT

IGLESIA DE SAN GERVASIO

CASA TIA MICHA

PORTAL MAYA

FARMACIA YZA

MUSEO SAN ROQUE

SHARED TAXIS TO CANCUN

CASA DE LOS VENADOS

MEXIGO TOURS

PRODUCTOS SOSA

CONATO

CAFÉ INTERNET COMPUTER

Parque San Juan

IGLESIA SAN JUAN

CASA HAMACA GUESTHOUSE

TABERNA DE LOS FRAILES

IGLESIA Y EX-CONVENTO SAN BERNARDINO DE SIENA

CASA QUETZAL

Parque de Sisal

HOSPITAL GENERAL

0   200 yds
0   200 m

© AVALON TRAVEL

©LIZA PRADO

Valladolid's historic Iglesia de San Gervasio

churches in the Yucatán whose facade faces north instead of west.

Museo San Roque

A long, high-ceilinged room—this used to be a church—the **San Roque Museum** (Calle 41 btwn Calles 38 and 40, no phone, 9am-9pm Mon.-Fri., 8am-6pm Sat.-Sun., free) is a worthwhile stop, with history exhibits on Valladolid, many focusing on the Caste War and the beginning of the Mexican Revolution. Displays of local handicrafts are also notable. Signage is in Spanish only.

Palacio Municipal

On the 2nd floor of the **city hall** (7am-7pm daily, free) is a large balcony overlooking the central plaza, with four large paintings by local artist Manuel Lizama. The paintings depict events in Valladolid's history: pre-Hispanic communities, the city's founding, the Caste War, and the Mexican Revolution. It's not spectacular, but still something to see.

Cenote Zaci

Right in the middle of town, **Cenote Zaci** (Calle 36 btwn Calles 37 and 39, no phone, 8am-6pm daily, US$1.25 adult, US$0.80 child under 13) is a dark natural pool at the bottom of a huge cavern, with a bank of trees on one side and a path looping down from the entrance above. It's often pooh-poohed as inferior to cenotes at Dzitnup, but it's a perfectly peaceful and attractive spot, and a lot quicker and easier to get to. You may find leaves and pollen floating on the water's surface, but it's still great for swimming. To have the cenote to yourself, go midweek, or better yet right after closing time, entering through the restaurant (you can use their bathroom to change) instead of the main gates.

Mayapán Agave Distillery

Along Valladolid's northern ring road, two kilometers (1.2 miles) south of the Cancún toll highway, the artisanal **Mayapán Agave Distillery** (Libremiento Nte., tel. 985/856-1727, www.mayapan.mx, 7am-6pm Mon.-Fri.,

decorative objects created by some of the most talented contemporary artisans from across Mexico, and the work usually incorporates religious, indigenous, or cultural themes. The museum is a labor of love, with all donations benefiting a local volunteer-run medical clinic and the Lions Club.

Iglesia de San Gervasio

Overlooking the central plaza, the **San Gervasio Church** (Calle 41 at Calle 42, no phone) has a sober Franciscan style. It was originally built in 1545 but in 1705 was deemed profaned and ordered demolished by the local bishop as the result of a political rivalry that involved the storming of the church, the desanctifying of its altar, and the death of four politicians. (The incident is now known as *El Crimen de los Alcaldes*, or The Mayors' Crime.) The church was rebuilt a year later, but its orientation changed so that the new altar would not be in the same position as the prior—indeed, the Iglesia de San Gervasio is one of the only colonial-era

ARCHAEOLOGICAL ZONES

7am-1pm Sat., US$2.50) leads visitors on half-hour tours that take in its agave fields and warehouse-size facility, detailing the traditional steps used to ferment, mash by horse-drawn mill, and distill the agave plant into liquor. They can't call it tequila because it's not made in Jalisco, but your taste buds might not be so finicky. Tours conclude with three different tastings and a subtle nudge toward the gift shop. English tours are available.

Cenotes de Dzitnup

Four kilometers (2.5 miles) west of Valladolid on Highway 180 is the small community of Dzitnup, home to two appealing underground cenotes. Both make for a unique and refreshing swim—and on warm days you may find them somewhat crowded. Both share a ticket kiosk and a large parking lot. Many small *artesanía* stands sit at the entrance, and you'll be aggressively pursued by children offering to watch your car or sell you a postcard.

Although the two are across the street from each other, **Cenote Xkeken** (no phone, 8am-5pm daily, US$5.50 adult, US$2 under 17, video cameras US$2.50) has been open longer and is better known; many postcards and travel guides call it "Cenote Dzitnup." After a reasonably easy descent underground (in a few places you must bend over because of a low ceiling; there's a hanging rope to help), you'll come to a circular pond of clear, cool water. It's a pretty, albeit damp, place, with a high dome ceiling that has one small opening at the top letting in a ray of sun and dangling green vines. Often an errant bird can be seen swooping low over the water before heading to the sun and sky through the tiny opening. Stalactites and at least one large stalagmite adorn the ceiling and cenote floor.

At **Cenote Samula** (no phone, 8:30am-5pm daily, US$5.50 adult, US$2 under 17, video cameras US$2.50), tree roots dangle impressively from the cavern roof all the way down to the water. You enter through a narrow tunnel, which opens onto a set of stairs that zigzag down to the water. Fearless kids jump from the stairs into the clear turquoise water below.

Many people ride bikes here, following a paved path that runs parallel to the highway. A cab to the cenotes runs about US$5.

Tours

For small group **van tours** packing in local and regional attractions, **MexiGo Tours** (Calle 43 btwn Calles 40 and 42, tel. 985/856-0777, www.mexigotours.com) is highly recommended. Its "Flamingo" excursion (US$85 pp) visits Río Lagartos, Ek' Balam, and the cake-like 17th-century church in nearby Uayma; another popular outing visits Chichén Itzá and Izamal, with a stop for a dip at the dreamy Yokdzonot cenote (US$85). Both these tours include breakfast, lunch, and transportation, but not site entrance fees. There's a minimum of three people or it's an extra US$25 per person.

ENTERTAINMENT AND EVENTS

Taking the cue from Mérida's successful weekly celebrations, Sundays here now feature a year-round cultural event called **Domingo Vallisoletano.** From 10am until about 8:30pm, the city closes the streets around the central plaza for artisan expositions, *trova* balladeers, folkloric dancing, and programs for kids. The tourist office also leads free hour-long tours of the area around the plaza at 11am, 1pm, and 4pm, though you may want to confirm these times.

Every January 27-February 2, Valladolid celebrates its patron saint, La Virgen de la Candelaria, in the **Expo-Feria Valladolid.** It's a blowout outdoor festival, where you'll be sure to see bullfights, rodeos, musical entertainment, and lots of food stands selling local delicacies and heart-stopping goodies. Venues vary; ask at the tourist office or your hotel for details.

SHOPPING

A tranquil courtyard of workshops and stores, the **Centro Artesanal Zaci** (Calle 39 btwn Calles 40 and 42, 7am-10pm daily) showcases local Maya women who make and sell their *huipiles* and hand-stitched blouses on-site. For a wider number of offerings, the **Mercado de Artesanías** (Calle 39 at Calle 44, 8am-8pm Mon.-Sat., 8am-2pm Sun.) has a decent variety of *guayaberas,* embroidered *huipiles,* hammocks, and other popular handicrafts. The selection isn't very large—there are only about a dozen shops here—so be sure to bargain. If you're interested in high-end Mexican handicrafts and art, **Yalat** (Calle 41 btwn Calles 40 and 42, tel. 985/856-1969, 9am-8pm Mon.-Fri., 9am-7pm Sat.-Sun.) is worth a stop. It's pricey, but the quality and variety of the items sold is excellent.

A family-owned business still chugging away after more than 100 years, the unassuming shop of distiller **Productos Sosa** (Calle 42 btwn Calles 47 and 49, tel. 985/856-2142, 8:30am-1:30pm and 4pm-7:30pm Mon.-Fri., 8:30am-2:30pm Sat.) sells smooth sugar cane liquors infused with ingredients like mint or anise with honey.

ACCOMMODATIONS

Valladolid offers a good selection of simple and mid-range hotels. Most are convenient to the central plaza. All have free Wi-Fi and, except for the hostel, provide parking.

Under US$50

Cozy fan-cooled dormitories at **Hostel Candelaria** (Parque la Candelaria, Calle 35 btwn Calles 42 and 44, tel. 985/856-2267, www.hostelvalladolidyucatan.com, US$10 dorm, US$23-27 s/d with fan) have 10-14 beds sharing one bathroom, with a low-ceilinged women-only dorm and a roomier mixed dorm. What the dorms lack in space is more than made up for by a sprawling back garden thick with papaya trees and hibiscus, shading an al fresco kitchen and eating area and hammocks tucked in nooks with personal reading lights. Inside the colonial building, you'll find another kitchen, free computers, lockers—including some for charging electronics—and a TV room. Socialize with other travelers over the free continental breakfast, then rent a bicycle to tour the local cenotes.

Set around a grassy courtyard, **Hotel Zaci** (Calle 44 btwn Calles 37 and 39, tel. 985/856-2167, www.hotelzaci.com.mx, US$36-40 s with a/c, US$44-54 d with a/c) offers well-kempt ground-floor rooms with decorative details like stenciling and ironwork furnishings. The top two floors contain remodeled "premier" rooms, which boast flat-screen TVs and newer decor. But the difference between the two levels of rooms is pretty minimal—there's just better light on the upper floors. A small, clean pool is a nice plus.

US$50-100

Steps from the plaza yet still very quiet, the new five-room ◖ **Casa Tía Micha** (Calle 39 btwn Calles 38 and 40, 985/856-2957, www.casatiamicha.com, US$70-105 s/d with a/c) is run by the great-grandchildren of the former owner. Stately wooden doors, rainforest showerheads, wrought-iron or carved headboards, and vintage furniture can be found throughout, and one of the more luxurious upstairs rooms boasts a decadent Jacuzzi tub. A full breakfast is served in the tranquil fruit tree garden, near the old *pozo* (well).

A converted 17th-century home, **Hotel El Mesón del Marqués** (central plaza, Calle 39 btwn Calles 40 and 42, tel. 985/856-2073, www.mesondelmarques.com, US$61 s/d standard with a/c, US$75 s/d superior with a/c, US$116-196 s/d suite) boasts a free lobby computer, lush courtyards, a gurgling fountain, arches upon arches, and a verdant garden with an egg-shaped pool. Rooms are divided into three categories: standard, superior, and suite. The first two types are decorated similarly with heavy wood furniture, ironwork headboards, and brightly colored woven bedspreads—the main differences are that the standard is smaller, has old-school air conditioners, and clunky TVs. Suites have modern decor and amenities and updated bathrooms, and are spacious. Though the prices are a bit inflated, this is still one of the most comfortable places to stay in town.

Casa Quetzal (Calle 51 btwn Calles 50 and 52, tel. 985/856-4796, www.casa-quetzal. com, US$66-75 s/d) is a charming, well-run bed-and-breakfast a half block from the pretty San Bernardino de Siena church. Large, attractive, high-ceilinged rooms surround a pretty garden and swimming pool, while a community kitchen and lovely reading room—with high-quality Mexican artwork, especially from Oaxaca and Jalisco—lend a homey feel. All rooms have air-conditioning, cable TV, two double beds, and a hammock; ask for a room away from the street for less traffic noise. Free yoga classes take place in its dedicated salon twice daily. Breakfast gets good reviews, but is a bit pricey at US$8. The hotel is somewhat removed from the central plaza, but the 10-minute walk there—along Valladolid's iconic Calzada de los Frailes—is a pleasure itself.

US$100-150

◖ Casa Hamaca Guesthouse (Parque San Juan, Calle 49 at Calle 40, tel. 985/856-5287, www.casahamaca.com, US$110-125 s/d with a/c, US$150 quad with a/c) has a convenient and peaceful location, facing a quiet church plaza about five blocks south of the main square. A lush garden and small pool add to the tranquility, and the guesthouse is spacious and bright. The eight rooms vary in size and decor: The Tree Suite has rattan furnishings, the Earth Suite has ochre highlights, and all rooms have dramatic hand-painted murals. A hearty breakfast is included, and massages, facials, Maya cleansings, and other treatments can be arranged. With advance notice the proprietor can also help set up rewarding volunteer opportunities or Spanish classes. Casa Hamaca is wheelchair accessible, and rates dip about US$20 in low season.

FOOD

Located next to the bus station, **◖ Cafetería Squimoz** (Calle 39 near Calle 46, tel. 985/856-4156, 7am-11pm Mon.-Sat., 8am-4pm Sun., US$3.75-7.50) is well worth a stop even if you're not on your way out of town. Big breakfasts and sandwiches are the specialties, though the coffee drinks and to-die-for milkshakes shouldn't be overlooked. If you've got a sweet tooth, try the homemade flan.

Adjacent to the Iglesia y Ex-Convento San Bernardino de Siena, the low lighting, attentive service, and open-air *palapa* dining room at **Taberna de los Frailes** (Calle 49 at Calle 41A, tel. 985/856-0689, noon-11pm daily Nov.-Apr., 1pm-11pm May-Oct., US$7.50-12) set an elegant backdrop for a crowd-pleasing menu of creative Yucatecan mainstays, seafood cocktails, and a few vegetarian entrées like *chaya* tamales or risotto. Its upscale bar has some sofa seating and a terrace area shaded by a profuse canopy of passion fruit. The restaurant's proximity to the monastery cenote can draw the odd mosquito; ask the staff if you need repellent.

Bohemia is alive and well at **Conato** (Calle 40 btwn Calles 45 and 47, tel. 985/856-2586, 5:30pm-midnight Wed.-Mon., US$4.25-7), where religious iconography and images of Frida Kahlo clutter a dining room of family-style wooden tables set off by a colonial tile floor. Yucatecan-influenced chicken dishes, fresh salads, and serviceable pasta dishes have creative visual flourishes, and the govinda dessert crepes laced with cream and chocolate are almost too pretty to eat. Open until late, it's also a sociable place for drinks or coffee.

With tables on the lovely Parque Candelaria, **La Casa del Café Kaffé** (Calle 35 at Calle 44, tel. 985/856-2879, 9am-1pm and 7pm-10:30pm daily, US$2-3.50) is a fantastic place to get breakfast or a late-night snack. It's owned and run by a welcoming Chilean couple, and the menu features empanadas, quesadillas, sandwiches, fruit shakes, and a nice variety of coffee drinks. If you don't see what you crave on the menu, be sure to ask for it—meals often are made to order.

A gorgeous place to enjoy a meal, the restaurant at the **Hotel El Mesón del Marqués** (Calle 39 btwn Calles 40 and 42, tel. 985/856-2073, 7am-11pm daily, US$7.50-12.50) has an interior courtyard with a colonial-style fountain and masses of fuchsia-colored bougainvillea draped over the balconies. The menu is predominately Yucatecan, though there are a variety of international options. Good choices include scrambled eggs with *chaya, sopa de lima,* and *poc-chuc.*

El Bazar (parque central, Calle 39 at Calle 40, US$1.25-5) is a local food court with a dozen or so inexpensive eateries selling mostly premade Yucatecan specialties. Hours are variable, but all are open for breakfast and lunch. Food is hit or miss—take a look at the offerings and decide which looks the freshest. (If anything, avoid the tamales.) Better yet, order something off the menu that hasn't been sitting around, like scrambled eggs or *salbutes.*

For groceries, **Super Willy's** (Calle 39 btwn Calles 42 and 44, 7am-10pm daily) has a decent selection of fresh and canned foods.

INFORMATION AND SERVICES
Tourist Information
Try your best at prying some useful information from Valladolid's **tourist office** (Palacio Municipal, Calle 40 at Calle 41, tel. 985/856-2529, ext. 114, 9am-9pm daily). At the very least, you should be able to get a map or two, and English is spoken.

Emergency Services
If you need medical assistance, the modern new **Hospital General** (Av. Chan Yokdzonot, tel. 985/856-2883, 24 hours) is located 4.5 kilometers (2.8 miles) south of the *cuota* highway; for meds only, **Farmacia Yza** (Calle 41 near Calle 40, tel. 985/856-4018), just off the central plaza, is open 24 hours. The **police** (Parque Bacalar, Calle 41 s/n, 24 hours) can be reached at 985/856-2100 or toll-free at 066.

Money
On or near the central plaza, **HSBC** (Calle 41 btwn Calles 42 and 44, 9am-5pm Mon.-Fri., 9am-3pm Sat.), **Banamex** (Calle 41 btwn Calles 42 and 44, 9am-4pm Mon.-Fri.), and **Bancomer** (Calle 40 btwn Calles 39 and 41, 8:30am-4pm Mon.-Fri.) all have ATMs.

Media and Communications
A tiny **post office** (Calle 40 btwn Calles 39 and 41, 8am-4:30pm Mon.-Fri., 8am-1pm Sat.) sits on the central plaza. There's free Wi-Fi in the central plaza, and we assume that the signal's strongest where the laptop-toting teens congregate in front of the Palacio Municipal. For computer access, try **Café Internet Computer** (Calle 49 at Calle 42, 8am-11pm daily, US$0.75/hour) or **Phonet** (Calle 46 at Calle 41, 7am-midnight daily, US$0.70/hour), which also offers long-distance telephone service (US$0.50/minute to the United States and Canada, US$0.70/minute to the rest of the world).

Laundry
The bustling **Lavandería Luyso** (Calle 40 at Calle 33, 8am-8pm Mon.-Sat., 8am-3pm Sun.) charges US$0.80 per kilo (2.2 pounds) and offers next-day service only.

GETTING THERE AND AROUND
Bus
Valladolid's **bus terminal** (Calle 39 at Calle 46, tel. 985/856-3448) is an easy walk from the central plaza, or if you have a lot of bags, a cheap taxi ride.

Taxi
Taxis are relatively easy to flag down, especially around the central plaza, and typically cost US$1.50-2 around town.

Colectivos (shared vans) to Pisté and Chichén Itzá (US$2, 40 minutes) depart approximately every 30 minutes from Calle 39 near the ADO bus terminal, and those for Mérida (US$11, 2.5 hours) leave from the terminal. Shared taxis for Cancún (US$10, 2.5 hours) congregate at Calle 38 between Calles 39 and 41.

Car
If you arrive from the toll highway (*cuota*), you'll enter town via Calle 42 (and return on Calle 40). It's a sobering US$20 toll driving in from Cancún, US$12 from Mérida (Kantunil), and US$5 to Chichén Itzá. In the center, eastbound Calle 41 and westbound Calle 39 access the free highway (*libre*).

ARCHAEOLOGICAL ZONES

ARCHAEOLOGICAL ZONES

VALLADOLID BUS SCHEDULE

Departures from Valladolid's **bus station** (Calle 39 at Calle 46, tel. 985/856-3448) include:

DESTINATION	PRICE	DURATION	SCHEDULE
Campeche	US$23.50	4.5 hours	1:35pm
Cancún	US$7.50-12	3 hours	every 30-60 mins 6am-10:30pm
Chetumal	US$14	5 hours	5:30am, 7:30am, 2:30pm, and 8:30pm
Chichén Itzá	US$2-5	50 minutes	every 30-60 mins 6am-10:30pm
Chiquilá	US$7.50	3 hours	2:45am
Cobá	US$2.75	1 hour	8:30am, 9:30am, 2:45pm, and 5:15pm
Izamal	US$4.30	1.5 hours	12:50pm
Mérida	US$7.50-12.50	2.5 hours	every 30-60 mins 5:45am-9:15pm
Playa del Carmen	US$8.50-12	3 hours	8:30am, 9:30am, 10:05am, 12:05pm, 1:05pm, 2:45pm, 3:05pm, 5:15pm, 5:30pm, and 8:05pm
Tizimín	US$1.90	1 hours	every 30-75 mins 5:30am-9:15pm
Tulum	US$5.50-7	2 hours	9 departures 8:30am-8:05pm

To rent a car in town, **Portal Maya** (Calle 41 btwn Calles 38 and 40, tel. 985/856-2513, www.portalmayatours.com.mx) is your lone option; it also organizes tours.

Bicycle

Bikes can be rented at both **Refraccionaría de Bicicletas Silva** (Calle 44 btwn Calles 39 and 41, tel. 985/856-3667, 9am-6pm daily) and neighboring **Aguilar Sport** (Calle 44 No. 195 btwn Calles 39 and 41, tel. 985/856-2125, 8am-2pm and 4pm-7pm daily) for US$0.80 per hour or US$5 per day, and from **Hostel Candelaria** (Parque la Candelaria, Calle 35 btwn Calles 42 and 44, tel. 985/856-2267) for US$1.25 per hour or US$7 per day.

Ek' Balam

Ek' Balam, Maya for Black Jaguar, is a unique and fascinating archaeological site whose significance has only recently been revealed and appreciated. Serious restoration of Ek' Balam didn't begin until the mid-1990s, and it was then that an incredibly well-preserved stucco frieze was discovered, hidden under an innocuous stone facade near the top of the site's main pyramid. The discovery rocketed Ek' Balam into preeminence, first among Maya scholars and more slowly among travelers in the Yucatán, once the frieze was excavated and opened to the public. Much remains a mystery about Ek' Balam, but archaeologists believe it was founded around 300 BC and became an important commercial center, its influence peaking in AD 700-1100.

Ek' Balam sees a fraction of the tourists that visit other Maya sites, despite being just 30 kilometers (19 miles) north of Valladolid and in close proximity to both Cancún and Mérida. Though the one-lane access road is riddled with potholes, the ruins and the adjacent cenote are an easy jaunt from Valladolid. Ek' Balam is small enough that even an hour is enough to appreciate its treasures, and it's a tranquil place that doesn't get besieged by mammoth tour groups.

The **village** of Ek' Balam is two kilometers (1.2 miles) from the ruins, with two good options for accommodations and food; for more options and other traveler services, head to Valladolid.

◖ EK' BALAM ARCHAEOLOGICAL ZONE

Entering **Ek' Balam** (8am-5pm daily, US$8), you'll pass through a low thick wall and an elegant corbeled arch. Walls are rare in Maya cities, and were most commonly used for defense, as in the cases of Becán and Tulum. Ek' Balam's low thick walls would not have slowed marauding rivals, however, and so they most likely served to enforce social divisions, with some areas off-limits (but not out of view!) to all but the elite. They may also have been decorative—the city possessed great aesthetic flair, as the entry arch and the famous stucco frieze demonstrate.

Acrópolis and El Trono

The highlight of Ek' Balam is an artful and remarkably pristine stucco frieze known as **El Trono** (The Throne), located under a protective *palapa* roof two-thirds of the way up Ek' Balam's main pyramid, the **Acrópolis.** A steep stairway leads up the center of the pyramid, and a platform to the left of the stairs provides visitors a close-up view of El Trono.

About 85 percent of El Trono is the original stucco. Often structures like this would have been painted blue or red, but not so here. In fact, shortly after it was built, El Trono was sealed behind a stone wall 50-60 centimeters (19-24 inches) thick. It remained there untouched until the 1990s, when restoration workers accidentally—and fortuitously—dislodged one of the protective stones, revealing the hidden chamber beneath.

The tall, winged figures immediately catch your eye, as they appear so much like angels. In fact, they are high priests. Notice that one is deformed—his left arm is longer than the right, and has only four fingers. The Maya considered birth defects to be a sign of divinity, and the priest depicted here may have risen to his position precisely because of his deformation.

Directly over the door is a seated figure (unfortunately, the head is missing). This represents Ukit Kan Le'k Tok', one of Ek' Balam's former rulers, described in inscriptions as the "king of kings," and the person for whom El Trono was built and dedicated. A tomb was discovered in the chamber behind the frieze, containing thousands of jade, gold, obsidian, and ceramic artifacts left as offerings to this

EK' BALAM ARCHAEOLOGICAL ZONE

ACRÓPOLIS

EL TRONO

INNER WALL

OUTER WALL

STRUCTURE II

North Plaza

STRUCTURE III

BALL COURT

South Plaza

LAS GEMELAS

STRUCTURE X

LA RODONDA

INNER WALL

OUTER WALL

OUTER WALL

SACBÉ

SACBÉ

ENTRANCE

SCALE NOT AVAILABLE

© AVALON TRAVEL

powerful leader. The small face at the king-figure's navel represents a rival whom he defeated in war.

Viewed as a whole, the frieze is unmistakably a Chenes-style monster mouth: a huge stylized mask in which the doorway represents the gaping mouth of a high god. The pointed upper and lower teeth are easy to spot, as are the spiral eyes. Monster mouths are never mundane, but this one is especially elaborate: Notice how two beautifully crafted figures straddle the lower eyelids, while hoisting the upper lids with their shoulders. At least five more figures, plus lattice patterns and other designs, adorn the rest of the mask.

Before heading down, climb the rest of the way to the top of the Acrópolis for a panoramic vista. At 32 meters (105 feet) high and 158 meters (515 feet) wide, the Acrópolis is bigger than Chichén Itzá's main pyramid, and in fact is one of the largest Maya pyramids ever built, a detail that's often overlooked amid the excitement surrounding El Trono. The scene from atop is memorable; with the exception of the odd telephone and radio tower, and the site's visitors center, the view of the broad Yucatecan

© LIZA PRADO

Ek' Balam's remarkable stucco frieze, known as El Trono (The Throne)

(The Twins), known as Structure 17. As the plaque indicates, these identical structures are perhaps the best example of Ek' Balam's particular architectural style. Having perfected the use of stucco, Ek' Balam's builders did not concern themselves with precise masonry, as the stones would be covered in a thick stucco cap. However, stucco proved much less resilient to erosion, and centuries later the structures here appear shabbier than even much older ones, like in Campeche's Río Bec region, where stucco was less common and stone blocks were more carefully cut and fitted. Recent excavations have focused on these two buildings, where intriguing freehand marks and paintings—perhaps akin to graffiti today—have been discovered.

Practicalities

Ek' Balam is open 8am-5pm daily; general admission is US$8, use of video US$4. Guides can be hired at the entrance to the ruins (US$50, 1-1.5 hours, available in Spanish or English). French- and Italian-speaking guides are sometimes available.

CENOTE X'CANCHÉ

A short distance from the Ek' Balam archaeological site, **Cenote X'Canché** (cell. tel. 985/100-9915, www.ekbalam.com.mx, 8am-4pm daily, US$4) is an excellent community-run ecotourism project, and a must-do add-on to a ruins visit. From Ek' Balam's parking area, a dirt road winds 1.5 kilometers (0.9 mile) through low dense forest to the cenote, which is 14 meters (46 feet) deep and nearly circular, with sheer walls and tree roots descending picturesquely to cool, clean water. A wooden staircase leads to the water's edge, great for swimming. It's a pleasant shaded walk in, though many visitors rent bikes (US$6 for 3 hours) or take advantage of the on-site bike taxis (US$4 pp round-trip). Facilities include restrooms, shower and changing areas, a restaurant, *palapa*-shaded hammocks for reading and hanging out, and comfortable overnight accommodations. Rappelling from the cenote edge or ziplining across it can each be arranged

landscape is probably not all that different than the one Maya priests and kings enjoyed from this very same vantage point more than a thousand years ago.

South Plaza

Descending the pyramid, you can see that Ek' Balam is a fairly small site, with two mid-size plazas (north and south), a ball court in the middle, and its main structures crowded together.

On the south side of the south plaza stands **La Rodonda**, or the Oval Palace. A squat mid-size structure, La Rodonda has an eclectic array of overlapping lines and curves, stairs, and terraces. It underwent numerous iterations, as did virtually all Maya temples, but the result here was especially eclectic. Archaeologists suspect La Rodonda was used for astronomical observations, and the discovery of several richly adorned tombs suggest it had a ceremonial purpose as well.

Flanking La Redonda are **Las Gemelas**

Near the ruins of Ek' Balam, Cenote X'Canché makes for a splendid swim.

for an additional fee (US$8-30, half price child under 12); there's also an admission package (US$25) that includes both those activities plus bicycle rental.

ACCOMMODATIONS

In the Maya village near the ruins, **◖ Genesis Retreat Ek' Balam** (cell. tel. 985/101-0277 or 985/100-4805, www.genesisretreat.com, US$50-70 s/d, US$80 family unit) has nine rooms and *cabañas* set on a leafy enclosed property with a natural bio-filtered pool in the middle. Three units share a large clean bathroom, the others have private bathrooms, one has air-conditioning, and all are different in style and decor. One of the favorites, the Birdhouse, has screen windows on all sides and a small balcony overlooking the pool and garden. There's real environmental commitment at work here: Recycled materials were used in construction, its 101-hectare (250-acre) organic farm provides most of the produce for its meals, and there's a solar hot-water system and extensive

greywater reuse on the property. The hard-working Canadian owner offers tours of the village and local artisan workshops (US$15 pp, minimum 4 people), and is involved in a number of educational projects around town. Be aware that a number of friendly pooches lounge about the property—fine if you like dogs, but not everyone's thing—and that the property closes during September. Morning pastries and coffee are included, and full breakfasts and dinner are available. There's Internet access, and skilled work/lodging exchanges (2-week minimum) are negotiable.

Dolcemente Ek' Balam (cell. tel. 985/106-8083, www.fincacasaazul.com.mx/ekbalam.htm, US$50/71 d/t, US$62 s/d with a/c) doesn't compete with Genesis for Zen or eco-ambience; it's simply a nice comfortable hotel. Spacious rooms have tile floors, okay beds, private hot-water bathrooms, and fans (except for two rooms with air-conditioning). Upstairs units have higher ceilings and better ventilation—making them worth requesting—and all look onto the hotel's peaceful garden.

Recently completed, **Cenote X'Canché** (cell. tel. 985/100-9915, www.ekbalam.com.mx, US$38 s/d/t) rents three well-built and solar-powered *palapa cabañas* near the cenote, each with queen bed and a hammock (plus mosquito nets). The windows have good screens, and there's hot water and a fan. A three-course lunch or dinner at its restaurant costs US$8; breakfast is US$7.

FOOD

All the accommodations above have restaurants. Genesis Retreat Ek' Balam's restaurant **Chaya's Natural Restaurant** (cell. tel. 985/101-0277 or 985/100-4805, www.genesisretreat.com, US$8.50-12) serves breakfast and dinner to its guests, but is open to the public for lunch. Terrific vegetarian and vegan meals are prepared with organic produce grown on the owner's nearby farm.

Dolcemente Ek' Balam (cell. tel. 985/106-8083, www.fincacasaazul.com.mx/ekbalam.htm, noon-11pm Tues.-Sun., US$7.50-12) specializes in Italian food, including fresh handmade ravioli, fettuccini, and other pasta. Its products are also 100 percent natural and organic, and meals are served in a large, tasteful dining room.

GETTING THERE AND AROUND
Car
From Valladolid, drive north on Highway 295 toward Tizimín for about 17 kilometers (10.5 miles), past the town of Temozón, to a well-marked right-hand turnoff to Ek' Balam. From there, drive another 11 kilometers (6.8 miles)

to an intersection: Turn left to reach the village and accommodations, or continue straight to reach the archaeological site.

Taxi
Colectivo (shared) taxis from Valladolid to the village of Ek' Balam leave from a stop on Calle 44 between Calles 35 and 37 (US$3); mornings have the most frequent departures. Otherwise, a private taxi costs about US$13 for up to four people. If you're planning on visiting the ruins only, you can often negotiate with the driver to wait there for a couple of hours and bring you back for around US$25.

Cobá

The Maya ruins of Cobá make an excellent complement—or even alternative—to the memorable but vastly overcrowded ruins at Tulum. Cobá doesn't have Tulum's stunning Caribbean view and beach, but its structures are much larger and more ornate—in fact, Cobá's main pyramid is the second tallest in the Yucatán Peninsula, and it's one of few you are still allowed to climb. The ruins are also surrounded by lakes and thick forest, making it a great place to see birds, butterflies, and tropical flora.

◼ COBÁ ARCHAEOLOGICAL ZONE
Cobá (8am-5pm daily, US$4) is especially notable for the complex system of *sacbeob*, or raised stone causeways, that connected to other cities, near and far. (The term *sacbeob*—whose singular form is *sacbé*—means white roads.) Dozens of such roads crisscross the Yucatán Peninsula, but Cobá has more than any other city, underscoring its status as a commercial, political, and military hub. One road extends in an almost perfectly straight line from the base of Cobá's principal pyramid to the town of Yaxuna, more than 100 kilometers (62 miles) away—no small feat considering a typical *sacbé* was 1-2 meters (3.3-6.6 feet) high and about

4.5 meters (15 feet) wide, and covered in white mortar. In Cobá, some roads were even bigger—10 meters (32.8 feet) across. In fact, archaeologists have uncovered a massive stone cylinder believed to have been used to flatten the broad roadbeds.

History
Cobá was settled as early as 100 BC around a collection of small lagoons; it's a logical and privileged location, as the Yucatán Peninsula is virtually devoid of rivers, lakes, or any other aboveground water. Cobá developed into an important trading hub, and in its early existence had a particularly close connection with the Petén region of present-day Guatemala. That relationship would later fade as Cobá grew more intertwined with coastal cities like Tulum, but Petén influence is obvious in Cobá's high steep structures, which are reminiscent of those in Tikal. At its peak, around AD 600-800, Cobá was the largest urban center in the northern lowlands, with some 40,000 residents and over 6,000 structures spread over 50 square kilometers (31 square miles). The city controlled most of the northeastern portion of the Yucatán Peninsula during the same period before being toppled by the Itzás of Chichén Itzá following a protracted war in

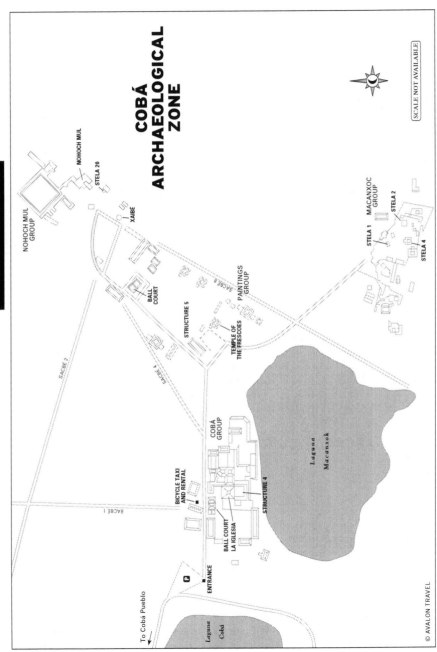

COBÁ ARCHAEOLOGICAL ZONE

SCALE NOT AVAILABLE

NOHOCH MUL

NOHOCH MUL GROUP

STELA 20

XAIBÉ

BALL COURT

STRUCTURE 5

SACBE 8

PAINTINGS GROUP

TEMPLE OF THE FRESCOES

MACANXOC GROUP

STELA 1

STELA 2

STELA 4

SACBE 2

SACBE 4

COBÁ GROUP

BICYCLE TAXI AND RENTAL

SACBE 1

STRUCTURE 4

BALL COURT

LA IGLESIA

Laguna Macanxok

ENTRANCE

To Cobá Pueblo

Laguna Cobá

© AVALON TRAVEL

the mid-800s. Following a widespread Maya collapse—of which the fall of Cobá was not the cause, though perhaps an early warning sign—the great city was all but abandoned, save as a pilgrimage and ceremonial site for the ascendant Itzás. It was briefly reinhabited in the 12th century, when a few new structures were added, but had been abandoned again, and covered in a blanket of vegetation, by the time of the Spanish conquest.

Cobá Group

Passing through the entry gate, the first group of ruins you encounter is the Cobá Group, a collection of over 50 structures and the oldest part of the ancient city. Many of Cobá's *sacbeob* initiate here. Its primary structure, **La Iglesia** (The Church), rises 22.5 meters (74 feet) from a low platform, making it Cobá's second-highest pyramid. The structure consists of nine platforms stacked atop one another and notable for their round corners. Built in numerous phases beginning in the Early Classic era, La Iglesia is far more reminiscent of Tikal and other Petén-area structures than it is of the long palaces and elaborate facades typical of Puuc and Chenes sites. Visitors are no longer allowed to climb the Iglesia pyramid due to the poor state of its stairs, but it is crowned with a small temple where archaeologists discovered a cache of jade figurines, ceramic vases, pearls, and conch shells.

The Cobá Group also includes one of the city's two **ball courts**, and a large acropolis-like complex with wide stairs leading to raised patios. At one time these patios were connected, forming a long gallery of rooms that likely served as an administrative center. The best-preserved structure in this complex, **Structure 4,** has a long vaulted passageway beneath its main staircase; the precise purpose of this passageway is unclear, but it's a common feature in Cobá and affords a close look at how a so-called Maya Arch is constructed.

The Cobá Group is directly opposite the stand where you can rent bicycles or hire bike taxis. Many travelers leave it for the end of their visit, after they've turned in their bikes.

Nohoch Mul Group

From the Cobá Group, the path winds nearly two kilometers (1.2 miles) through dense forest to Cobá's other main group, Nohoch Mul. The name is Yucatec Maya for Big Mound—the group's namesake pyramid rises an impressive 42 meters (138 feet) above the forest floor, the equivalent of 12 stories. (It was long believed to be the Yucatán Peninsula's tallest structure until the main pyramid at Calakmul in Campeche was determined to be some 10 meters higher.) Like La Iglesia in the Cobá Group, Nohoch Mul is composed of several platforms with rounded corners. A long central staircase climbs steeply from the forest floor to the pyramid's lofty peak. A small temple at the top bears a fairly well-preserved carving of the Descending God, an upside-down figure that figures prominently at Tulum but whose identity and significance is still unclear. (Theories vary widely, from Venus to the God of Bees.)

Nohoch Mul is one of few Maya pyramids

The view from atop Cobá's highest pyramid, Nohoch Mul, is spectacular, but be sure to watch your step!

that visitors are still allowed to climb, and the view from the top is impressive—a flat green forest spreading almost uninterrupted in every direction. A rope running down the stairs makes going up and down easier.

Where the path hits Nohoch Mul is **Stela 20,** positioned on the steps of a minor structure, beneath a protective *palapa* roof. It is one of Cobá's best-preserved stelae, depicting a figure in an elaborate costume and headdress, holding a large ornate scepter in his arms—both signifying that he is an *ahau,* or high lord or ruler. The figure, as yet unidentified, is standing on the backs of two slaves or captives, with another two bound and kneeling at his feet. Stela 20 is also notable for the date inscribed on it—November 30, 780—the latest Long Count date yet found in Cobá.

Xaibé and the Ball Court

Between the Cobá and Nohoch Mul Groups are several smaller but still significant structures. Closest to Nohoch Mul is a curiously conical structure that archaeologists have dubbed **Xaibé,** a Yucatec Maya word for crossroads. The name owes to the fact that it's near the intersection of four major *sacbeob,* and for the same reason, archaeologists believe it may have served as a watchtower. That said, its unique design and imposing size suggest a grander purpose. Round structures are fairly rare in Maya architecture, and most are thought to be astronomical observatories; there's no evidence Xaibé served that function, however, particularly since it lacks any sort of upper platform or temple. Be aware that the walking path does not pass Xaibé—you have to take the longer bike path to reach it.

A short distance from Xaibé is the second of Cobá's **ball courts.** Both courts have imagery of death and sacrifice, though they are more pronounced here: a skull inscribed on a stone in the center of the court, a decapitated jaguar on a disc at the end, and symbols of Venus (which represented death and war) inscribed on the two scoring rings. This ball court also had a huge plaque implanted on one of its slopes,

with over 70 glyphs and dated AD 465; the plaque in place today is a replica, but the original is under a *palapa* covering at one end of the court, allowing visitors to examine it more closely.

Paintings Group

The Paintings Group is a collection of five platforms encircling a large plaza. The temples here were among the last to be constructed in Cobá and pertain to the latest period of occupation, roughly AD 1100-1450. The group's name comes from paintings that once lined the walls, though very little color is visible now, unfortunately. Traces of blue and red can be seen in the upper room of the **Temple of the Frescoes,** the group's largest structure, but you aren't allowed to climb up to get a closer look.

Although centrally located, the Paintings Group is easy to miss on your way between the more outlying pyramids and groups. Look for a sign for **Structure 5,** where you can leave your bike (if you have one) and walk into the group's main area.

Macanxoc Group

From the Paintings Group, the path continues southeasterly for about a kilometer (0.6 mile) to the Macanxoc Group. Numerous stelae have been found here, indicating it was a place of great ceremonial significance. The most famous of these monuments is **Stela 1,** aka the Macanxoc Stela. It depicts a scene from the Maya creation myth—"the hearth stone appears"—along with a Long Count date referring to a cycle ending the equivalent of 41.9 billion, billion, billion years in the future. It is the most distant Long Count date known to have been conceived and recorded by the ancient Maya. Stela 1 also has reference to December 21, 2012, when the Maya Long Count completed its first Great Cycle, equivalent to 5,125 years. Despite widespread reports to the contrary, there is no known evidence, at Cobá or anywhere, that the Maya believed (much less predicted) that the world would end on that date.

Deciphering the Glyphs

For years, scholars could not agree whether the fantastic inscriptions found on Maya stelae, codices, and temple walls were anything more than complex records of numbers and dates. Many thought the text was not "real writing," as it did not appear to reproduce spoken language. Even those who believed the writing to be more meaningful despaired at ever reading it.

Mayanist and scholar Michael D. Coe's *Breaking the Maya Code* (Thames and Hudson, 1992) is a fascinating account of the decipherment of Maya hieroglyphics. Coe describes how, in 1952, reclusive Russian scholar Yuri Valentinovich Knorosov made a crucial breakthrough by showing that Maya writing did in fact convey spoken words. Using a rough alphabet recorded by Fray Diego de Landa (the 16th-century bishop who, ironically, is best known for having destroyed numerous Maya texts), Knorosov showed that ancient texts contain common Yucatec Maya words such as *cutz* (turkey) and *tzul* (dog). Interestingly, Knorosov conducted his research from reproductions only, having never held a Maya artifact or visited an ancient temple. (When he did finally visit Tikal in 1990, Coe says Knorosov wasn't very impressed.)

But Knorosov's findings were met with staunch resistance by some of the field's most influential scholars, which delayed progress for decades. By the mid-1980s, however, decipherment picked up speed; one of many standouts from that era is David Stuart, the son of Maya experts, who went to Cobá with his parents at age eight and passed the time copying glyphs and learning Yucatec Maya words from local playmates. As a high school student he served as chief epigrapher on a groundbreaking exploration in Belize, and at age 18 he received a US$128,000 MacArthur Fellowship (aka "Genius Award") to, as he told Michael Coe, "play around with the glyphs" full-time.

Researchers now know that Maya writing is like most other hieroglyphic systems. What appears at first to be a single glyph can have up to four parts, and the same word can be expressed in pictorial, phonetic, or hybrid form. Depending on context, one symbol can have either a pictorial or phonetic role; likewise, a particular sound can be represented in more than one way. The word *cacao* is spelled phonetically as "ca-ca-u" but is written with a picture of a fish (*ca*) and a comb-like symbol (also *ca*, according to Landa) and followed by -u. One of David Stuart's great insights was that for all its complexity, much of Maya glyphic writing is "just repetitive."

But how do scholars know what the symbols are meant to sound like in the first place? Some come from the Landa alphabet, others are suggested by the pictures that accompany many texts, still others from patterns derived by linguistic analyses of contemporary Maya languages. In some cases, it is simply a hunch that, after applying it to a number of texts, turns out to be right. If this seems like somewhat shaky scientific ground, it is—but not without a means of being proved. The cacao decipherment was confirmed when the same glyph was found on a jar with cacao residue still inside.

Hundreds of glyphs have been deciphered, and most of the known Maya texts can be reliably translated. The effort has lent invaluable insight into Maya civilization, especially dynastic successions and religious beliefs. Some archaeologists lament, not unreasonably, that high-profile glyphic studies divert attention from research into the lives of everyday ancient Maya, who after all far outnumbered the nobility but are not at all represented in the inscriptions. That said, it's impossible not to marvel at how one of the world's great ancient civilizations is revealed in the whorls and creases of fading stone pictures.

ARCHAEOLOGICAL ZONES

Flora and Fauna

The name Cobá (Water Stirred by the Wind in Maya) is surely a reference to the group of shallow lagoons here (Cobá, Macanxoc, Xkanha, and Sacakal). The archaeological site and the surrounding wetlands and forest are rich with birdlife—herons, egrets, motmot, parrots, and the occasional toucan are not uncommon. Arrive early to see the most birds—at the very least you'll get an earful of their varied songs and cries. Later, as the temperature climbs, you'll start to see myriad colorful butterflies, including the large, deep-blue morphidae and the bright yellow-orange barred sulphur.

If you look on the ground, you'll almost certainly see long lines of leaf-cutter ants. One column carries freshly cut leaves to the burrow, and the other marches in the opposite direction, empty-jawed, returning for more. The vegetation decays in their nests, and the fungus that grows on the compost is an important staple of the ants' diet—a few scientists even claim that this makes leaf-cutter ants the world's second species of agriculturists. Only particular types of leaves will do, and the columns can be up to a kilometer (0.6 mile) long.

Practicalities

Cobá's main groups are quite spread apart, and visiting all of them adds up to several kilometers. Fortunately, you can rent a bicycle (US$3) or hire a *triciclo* (US$9 for 1 hour, US$15 for 2 hours) at a large stand a short distance past the entryway, opposite the Cobá Group. Whether you walk or ride, don't forget a water bottle, comfortable shoes, bug repellent, sunscreen, and a hat. Watch for signs and stay on the designated trails. Guide service is available—prices are not fixed but average US$52 per group (1.5 hours, up to 6 people). Parking at Cobá is US$4.

Cobá is not nearly as crowded as Tulum (and is much larger), but it's still a good idea to arrive as early as possible to beat the ever-growing crowds.

COBÁ PUEBLO

It's fair to say that the town of Cobá, a rather desultory little roadside community, has never regained the population or stature that it had as a Maya capital more than 1,000 years ago. Most travelers visit Cobá as a day trip from Tulum or Valladolid, or on a package tour from resorts on the coast. There are two decent hotels in town, used mostly by those who want to appreciate Cobá's rich birdlife, which means being at the gate right when the site opens at 8am; if you're lucky, the gatekeeper may even let you in early.

Sights

Cobá Pueblo itself doesn't have much in the way of sights—besides the ruins, of course—but a number of small eco-attractions have cropped up, all a short distance from town.

RESERVA DE MONOS ARAÑAS PUNTA LAGUNA

The **Punta Laguna Spider Monkey Reserve** (cell. tel. 985/107-9182, 7:30am-5:30pm daily, US$5) is a protected patch of forest that's home to various families of boisterous spider monkeys, as well as smaller groups of howler monkeys and numerous bird species. A short path winds through the reserve, passing a small unexcavated Maya ruin and a large lagoon where you can rent canoes (US$8.50). There's also a zipline and a place to rappel into a cenote, but it's typically reserved for large groups. Your best chance of spotting monkeys is by going in late afternoon, and by hiring one of the guides near the entrance (US$10 pp, minimum 2 people). The reserve (whose official name is Otoch Ma'ax Yetel Kooh, Yucatec Maya for House of the Spider Monkey and Puma) is operated by a local cooperative, whose members live in the nearby village and serve as guides; most speak at least some English. Be sure to wear good walking shoes and bring plenty of bug repellent. The reserve is located 18 kilometers (11 miles) north of Cobá, on the road toward Nuevo X'can.

Tropical Monkeys

The Yucatán is home to three types of monkeys: spider, howler, and black howler. Intelligent and endearing, these creatures are prime targets for the pet trade. They have been so hunted that today all three are in danger of extinction. Experts estimate that for every tropical monkey sold, three die during transportation and distribution. In an effort to protect these creatures, the Mexican government has prohibited their capture or trade. As you wander through the ruins of **Cobá** or through the **Punta Laguna Spider Monkey Reserve,** keep your ears perked and your eyes peeled. You're sure to see—or, at least, hear—them. Spider and howler monkeys are most active at sunrise and sundown; consider arriving early or staying late to increase your chances of spotting a few.

© LIZA PRADO

Howler monkeys are common in regional nature reserves.

◖ CENOTES

If you've got a car, a cluster of three well-maintained and well-run cenotes (no phone, 8am-5pm daily) are a great addition to a day spent at Cobá. **Choo-Ha, Tamcach-Ha,** and **Multun-Ha** are southwest of Cobá and are operated jointly (US$5/7/10 for 1/2/3 cenotes); a fourth cenote called **Nohoch-Ha** is a bit farther and requires a separate entrance fee (US$2). Each is slightly different—one has a high roof and platform for jumping, another is wide and low—but all are impressive enclosed chambers bristling with stalactites, filled with cool crystalline water that's heaven on a hot day. Cement or wooden stairways lead down to pools; showers and changing areas are available at Choo-Ha. To get there, continue past the Cobá ruins on the road to Tepich and follow the signs.

Accommodations

There are just two recommendable hotels in Cobá Pueblo; if both are booked, consider heading to Tulum or Valladolid, each about 45 minutes away by car or bus.

The low-key **Hotel Sac Be** (Calle Principal, tel. 984/206-7140 or cell. tel. 984/135-3097, US$29 s/d with fan, US$37.50 s/d with a/c) has friendly service and spotless rooms with one or two beds, televisions, old-school air conditioners, and a small desk. All have private bathrooms and open onto a long outdoor corridor. Guests get 10 percent off at the hotel restaurant (which is the small one right above the mini-mart reception area; the much larger attached restaurant has a different owner).

Somewhat overpriced but the only mid-range option in town, **Villas Arqueológicas Cobá** (facing Laguna Cobá, tel. 984/206-7000, toll-free Mex. tel. 800/557-7755, www.villasarqueologicas.com.mx, US$92 s/d with a/c) started out as a Club Med, believe it or not, but has since become an independent hotel. Rooms are oddly pod-like, sort of what staying in the space station must be like. They open onto a wide corridor that in turn surrounds a large, pleasant pool. The hotel restaurant serves good but overpriced meals. Units have air-conditioning—which helps with mustiness—but no TV; free Wi-Fi in the lobby area only.

Food

With a large raised patio overlooking the lagoon, **La Pirámide** (Calle Principal at Laguna Cobá, no phone, 7:30am-9pm daily, US$6-15) is a nice place for lunch après-ruins or beer and snacks in the evening. The restaurant receives a number of tour groups, and it often has a buffet set up (US$12.50); otherwise the menu has grilled fish, chicken, and meat dishes as well as typical Mexican fare.

A few doors down and just before the entrance to Villas Arqueológicas, **Nicte Ha** (facing Laguna Cobá, tel. 984/206-7025, 8am-7pm daily, US$3-8) is a small place serving tacos, enchiladas, and various pork dishes.

The restaurant at **Villas Arqueológicas Cobá** (facing Laguna Cobá, tel. 984/206-7000, toll-free Mex. tel. 800/557-7755, www.villasarqueologicas.com.mx, 7:30am-10pm daily, US$6-16) is comfortable and quiet, and has a decent selection of pasta, seafood, and Yucatecan dishes. It's pleasant, though a bit pricey.

Across the street from the church, **Abarrotes Neftalí** (Calle Principal s/n, 7am-11pm daily) is a mini-mart that sells canned goods, bread, and some fresh produce.

Information and Services

Cobá has neither an official tourist office nor a health clinic. There also are no banks or ATMs—the nearest banking and medical services are in Tulum and Valladolid.

Facing the lagoon, **Farmacia El Porvenir** (Calle Principal s/n, no phone, 9am-1pm and 2pm-9pm Mon.-Sat.) is a small shop selling basic medicines and toiletries.

The **police station** (toll-free tel. 066) is halfway down the main drag, before you hit the lagoon.

Getting There and Around

You can easily walk to any of the listed hotels, restaurants, and services in town; the archaeological site is a five-minute walk down the main road, alongside the lagoon.

BUS

A tiny bus station operates out of El Bocadito restaurant (Calle Principal). For the coast, the lone first-class bus departs Cobá at 3:10pm, with stops in Tulum (US$4, 1 hour), Playa del Carmen (US$7.75, 2.5 hours), and Cancún (US$12.25, 3.5 hours). Second-class buses to the same destinations cost a bit less but take longer; departures are at 9:30am, 10:30am, 1:30pm, 3:30pm, 4pm, and 6pm.

There are just two first-class buses headed inland, leaving Cobá at 10am and 7:45pm for Valladolid (US$3.25-5.50, 1 hour), with first-class connections to Chichén Itzá and Mérida available there. Second-class bus departures for the same route (US$2.75 to Valladolid, US$5.25 to Chichén Itzá, US$10.75 to Mérida) are at 8am, 9:30am, 11am, noon, 1pm, and 7pm; note that the 8:30am, 11am, and noon buses go to Valladolid only, with connections available there.

CAR

Getting to Cobá is easiest by car. No matter what direction you're coming from, the roads are smooth and scenic, cutting through pretty farmland and small towns. Keep your speed down, however, as there are innumerable *topes* (speed bumps) and occasional people and animals along the shoulder. Buses ply the same routes, but somewhat infrequently.

Three different roads lead to Cobá; none are named or marked, so they are known by the towns on either end. There are no formal services along any of the roads, save a gas station in the town of Chemax.

The Cobá-Tulum road (45 kilometers/28 miles) is the busiest, cutting southeast to Tulum and the coastal highway (Hwy. 307).

The other two roads connect to Highway 180, the main highway between Cancún and Chichén Itzá. The Cobá-Nuevo X'Can road (47 kilometers/29 miles) angles northeast, connecting with Highway 180 about 80 kilometers (50 miles) outside Cancún and passing places like the Punta Laguna monkey reserve along the way. The Cobá-Chemax road (30 kilometers/19 miles) angles northwest to the town of Chemax; from there it's another 20 kilometers (12.4 miles) to Valladolid and Highway 180, connecting to the highway about 40 kilometers (25 miles) from Chichén Itzá.

All three roads, plus the short access road to Cobá, intersect at a large roundabout just north of Cobá village. Pay close attention to which road you want to avoid a long detour.

ARCHAEOLOGICAL ZONES

www.moon.com

DESTINATIONS | ACTIVITIES | BLOGS | MAPS | BOOKS

MOON.COM is ready to help plan your next trip! Filled with fresh trip ideas and strategies, author interviews, informative travel blogs, a detailed map library, and descriptions of all the Moon guidebooks, Moon.com is all you need to get out and explore the world—or even places in your own backyard. While at Moon.com, sign up for our monthly e-newsletter for updates on new releases, travel tips, and expert advice from our on-the-go Moon authors. As always, when you travel with Moon, expect an experience that is uncommon and truly unique.

KEEP UP WITH MOON ON FACEBOOK AND TWITTER
JOIN THE MOON PHOTO GROUP ON FLICKR

MAP SYMBOLS

▦ Expressway	◖ Highlight	✘ Airfield	⚲ Golf Course
Primary Road	○ City/Town	✈ Airport	▯ Parking Area
Secondary Road	◉ State Capital	▲ Mountain	≋ Archaeological Site
Unpaved Road	✹ National Capital	✛ Unique Natural Feature	⛪ Church
------- Trail	★ Point of Interest		⛽ Gas Station
Ferry	• Accommodation	⚑ Waterfall	Glacier
Railroad	▼ Restaurant/Bar	▲ Park	Mangrove
Pedestrian Walkway	■ Other Location	▯ Trailhead	Reef
Stairs	Λ Campground	✗ Skiing Area	Swamp

CONVERSION TABLES

°C = (°F − 32) / 1.8
°F = (°C x 1.8) + 32
1 inch = 2.54 centimeters (cm)
1 foot = 0.304 meters (m)
1 yard = 0.914 meters
1 mile = 1.6093 kilometers (km)
1 km = 0.6214 miles
1 fathom = 1.8288 m
1 chain = 20.1168 m
1 furlong = 201.168 m
1 acre = 0.4047 hectares
1 sq km = 100 hectares
1 sq mile = 2.59 square km
1 ounce = 28.35 grams
1 pound = 0.4536 kilograms
1 short ton = 0.90718 metric ton
1 short ton = 2,000 pounds
1 long ton = 1.016 metric tons
1 long ton = 2,240 pounds
1 metric ton = 1,000 kilograms
1 quart = 0.94635 liters
1 US gallon = 3.7854 liters
1 Imperial gallon = 4.5459 liters
1 nautical mile = 1.852 km

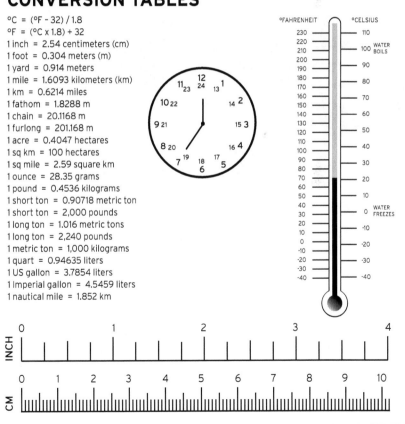

MOON SPOTLIGHT TULUM

Avalon Travel
a member of the Perseus Books Group
1700 Fourth Street
Berkeley, CA 94710, USA
www.moon.com

Editor and Series Manager: Kathryn Ettinger
Copy Editor: Ann Seifert
Graphics and Production Coordinator: Lucie Ericksen
Cover Designer: Kathryn Osgood
Map Editor: Kat Bennett
Cartographers: Chris Henrick, Kat Bennett,
  Kaitlin Jaffe

ISBN-13: 978-1-61238-888-5

Title page photo: one of Tulum's southern beaches
© Liza Prado

Printed in the United States

ABOUT THE AUTHORS

© LIZA PRADO

Gary Chandler

Gary Chandler grew up in a small ski town south of Lake Tahoe, California. He earned his bachelor's degree at UC Berkeley, and also studied abroad in Mexico City and Oaxaca. After graduation, Gary backpacked through much of Mexico and Central America, and later Southeast Asia, Europe, and the Caribbean. His first guidebook assignment was covering the highlands of Guatemala, which was followed by assignments in El Salvador, Honduras, Mexico, Brazil, the Dominican Republic, and elsewhere.

Gary has contributed to almost 30 guidebooks, many coauthored with wife and fellow travel writer/photographer Liza Prado. Between assignments, Gary earned a master's degree in journalism at Columbia University, worked as a news reporter and criminal investigator, and published numerous articles and blogs about travel in Latin America. He and Liza have two children and live in Colorado.

© GARY CHANDLER

Liza Prado

Liza Prado was working as a corporate attorney in San Francisco when she decided to take a leap of faith and try travel writing and photography. Ten years later, she has coauthored 18 guidebooks and written numerous feature stories and travel blogs to destinations throughout the Americas. Her photographs have been published by Moon Travel Guides and travel websites like Gogobot and Away.com.

Since her first visit to the region more than a decade ago, the Yucatán has remained one of Liza's favorite places to travel. For this assignment, she dived on coral reefs and snorkeled through cenotes, clambered on Maya ruins and paddled through mangroves, spied monkeys and tropical birds, explored beach towns and mega-resorts, caught a few local bands, and listened to rock-star DJs – all with two kids in tow (well, at least part of the time).

A graduate of Brown University and Stanford Law School, Liza currently lives in Denver, Colorado, with husband and coauthor Gary Chandler and their children, Eva and Leo.

About the Contributor

Beth Kohn is a freelance travel writer and photographer who specializes in Latin America and outdoor recreation. She has contributed to the *San Francisco Chronicle* and the BBC. She makes her home in San Francisco, California.